Memories
of
Portsmouth

Part of the
Memories
series

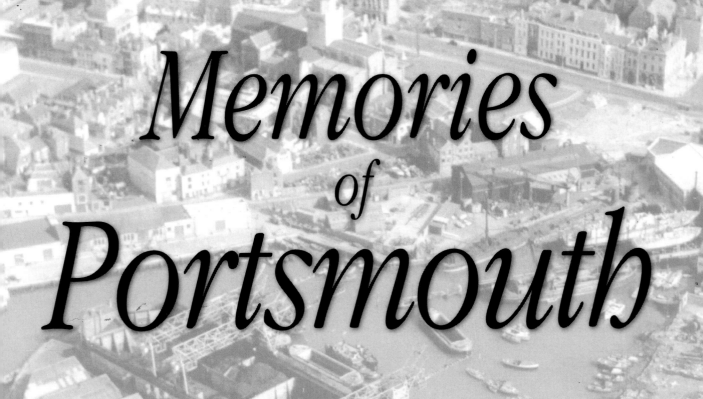

Memories
of
Portsmouth

*The Publishers would like to thank the following companies for supporting
the production of this book*

Main sponsor

Tremletts Chemists Limited

The Bridge Shopping Centre

FA Hendy & Lennox (Holdings) Limited

Portsmouth Housing Association

Zurich Insurance

First published in Great Britain by True North Books Limited
Units 3 - 5 Heathfield Industrial Park
Elland West Yorkshire
HX5 9AE
Tel. 01422 377977
© Copyright: True North Books Limited 1999

ISBN 1 900463 39 3

Text, design and origination by True North Books Limited
Printed and bound by The Amadeus Press Limited

Memories are made of this

Memories. We all have them: people, places and events, some good and some bad. Our memories of the place where we grew up are usually tucked away in a very special place in our mind. The best are probably connected with our childhood and youth, when we longed to be grown up and paid no attention to adults who told us to enjoy being young, as these were the best years of our lives. We look back now and realise that they were right.

Old photographs bring our memories flooding back - coronations and celebrations; talking pictures, Technicolour and television; the war years, rationing, and the shared hopes and fears which created such a warm community spirit; buying things made of nylon and plastic; fashions which took trouserbottoms and hemlines from drainpipes and mini-skirts to the other extreme; Doris Day, Acker Bilk, Elvis Presley and the Beatles; the jitterbug, the tango and discos; Ford Populars and Minis; decimalisation. Life changed so much over the years. Some changes were big, some small; some altered our lives in ways we never anticipated. Who in the early days of motoring could have foreseen the motorways and traffic systems of the latter decades of the 20th century? Did any of us realise, when we first saw a computer, what a tremendous impact they would have on our lives? Self-service supermarkets and frozen food made our lives easier - but at the expense of our friendly little corner shops. Nostalgia is always such a mixture of feelings . . . We hope that the collection of pictures in this book will remind you of happy days in bygone eras - and who knows, you might even have been there when one of the photographs was taken!

Contents

Portsmouth through the years

Nothing ever stays the same. Many would agree that as far as the town they grew up in is concerned, they could wish that it had, while others have welcomed the major redevelopments which so drastically changed the face of Portsmouth. But ever since King Richard I had a dock built here in 1194 for the maintenance of his ships, the town has never stood still.

It is the Royal Dock which has over the years influenced the fortunes of the city, and though the Dockyard is no longer what it was in its heyday, Portsmouth still acts as busy home base for many of the finest ships in the Royal Navy as well as providing shelter for warships from all over the world.

But the sea means more to Portsmouth than the docks only, as the many photographs reproduced here, of the promenade and beach at Southsea packed with happy holidaymakers, reminds us.

Many are the memories called to life within the pages of this book, from the magnificent Guildhall which rose from the ashes after World War II to the long-vanished shopping streets, replaced today by modern shopping malls and high-rise buildings. We are fortunate that the 20th century was so well chronicled, and this collection of fascinating images call to mind the town as it was 30, 50 and even 70 years ago.

We visit vanished cinemas such as the Gaiety and the luxurious Southsea Odeon, and magnificent theatres such the Theatre Royal and the King's in Southsea, which have been so well preserved - and take a peep at Pompey's finest hour, when Portsmouth FC lifted the FA Cup at Wembley in 1939.

This new collection reproduces these and many more nostalgic images to remind us of the way we once lived. We hope that you will read and enjoy 'Memories of Portsmouth' - and remember that history is still in the making.

Around the city centre

Christmas shopping; you either love it or hate it - but you still have to do it! A clock on the right tells us that the time is 9.55, and already the London Road shops, glittering with tinsel, Christmas trees and gifts, are attracting the punters - many, you will notice, wearing Royal Navy uniform. The Clarence would no doubt see some brisk trade come lunchtime! At least a good number of wives, mothers and sweethearts would be able to wake up to their gifts on Christmas Day.

High above the street (pictured in 1956) hang the seasonal illuminations, and it's obviously after dark that Portsmouth will come to brilliant life with hundreds of coloured lights that sparkle like gemstones in the darkness. At least the decorations in streets and shops would not have gone up until some time in November. In today's commercially-minded society, Christmas trees, coloured lights and elaborate decorations find their way into the shops around the end of September, along with the endless gifts we are expected to spend hundreds of pounds on. We would not wish for a return to the poverty that marked the early years of the 20th century, when Santa left few if any gifts in children's stockings - but oh, for a return to those simple, non-materialistic Christmases!

Above: The three well-known Portsmouth watering holes on the left of the photograph were an important part of many a seaman's pub crawl along Edinburgh Road: the Park Tavern on the extreme left, the Trafalgar Services Club next door, and adjoining it the Shipwrights' Arms, serving United Ales, as did the park Tavern. The view was snapped in 1958, but photographs which date from around the turn of the century reveal that Levy's were even then trading as quality tailors. At the time of this photograph, Levy's had closed their doors for the last time and the building had been sold. Note the canopy above the entrance to the Swiss Cafe nearby, lit by two elegant electric lamps which resemble torches, and the rather nice wrought ironwork of the canopy itself. Between the two buildings is the entrance to the Arcade, well known to the shoppers of Portsmouth. On the right Barclays Bank, surrounded by an exoskeleton of scaffolding and some extremely long and flimsy-looking ladders, is in the process of extensive restoration.

Above right: The stylised imperial lions gaze impassively over the square - and a number of passers-by gaze up at the newly rebuilt Guildhall in all its splendour. When the Guildhall was gutted during a heavy air raid on 10th January 1941, there were those who shook their heads and doubted that it could ever be rebuilt - the task seemed too great. A total of 300 enemy planes had concentrated their attentions on Portsmouth that day. During that one air raid the Luftwaffe dropped 25 incendiaries as well as high explosive bombs on the city, and when it was all over and the cost was counted, 171 people had lost their lives while 3,000 were homeless. However, the rebuilding programme eventually began, though there were many things, of course, which could never be replaced, such as the many fine paintings which before the raid had hung on the walls of the Great Hall. But on 8th June 1959 Her Majesty the Queen declared the new Guildhall officially open. It was a proud day for Portsmouth.

Landlords and landladies come and go, each making his mark or otherwise on a pub, but it is Mr 'Tiny' Dennis - all 30 stones of him - and his frail but formidable wife who are remembered when the Emperor of India is mentioned. In the late 1940s, it was Mrs Dennis who was the driving force behind the pub, which she managed while her over-large husband was working on his farm. It was said that this tiny woman was so well-respected that no man would ever use bad language in her hearing, and the Emperor of India was widely known as a very respectable establishment.

In front of the pub, the services of this white-coated police officer on point duty in Commercial Road would seem to be rather redundant. Point duty must have demanded a high concentration of manpower, however, and it was no doubt argued that instead of directing the town's traffic the police force would be better employed in concentrating their efforts on the fight against crime. So a few at a time they departed, leaving the motorist with a legacy of traffic lights to contend with at each junction. Traffic lights, while no doubt keeping the traffic flowing smoothly through the city centre (in theory at least), somehow lack the personal touch provided by the good old British bobby.

Shopping for the family each day was once a part of every housewife's life, especially in the days before refrigerators became a standard piece of equipment in every woman's kitchen. As we can see from the photograph, snapped in Fratton Road, it was also a time for catching up on the latest piece of news. Though the kiddies might not have been so keen on shopping it at least gave their mothers - few of whom would have thought of working at a full time job - the vital contact with other adults that kept them sane. The 165ft-high tower of St Mary's stands tall on the skyline; Christ has been worshipped on this spot since the 12th century in a succession of churches. The church

Events of the 1930s

HOT OFF THE PRESS

The years of the 1930s saw Adolf Hitler's sickening anti-Jewish campaign echoed in the streets of Britain. On 19th October 1936 Oswald Mosley's 7,000-strong British Union of Fascists clashed head on with thousands of Jews and Communists in London, resulting in 80 people being injured in the ensuing battle. Mosley and his 'blackshirts' later rampaged through the streets beating up Jews and smashing the windows of their businesses.

GETTING AROUND

At the beginning of the decade many believed that the airship was the transport of the future. The R101 airship, however, loaded with thousands of cubic metres of hydrogen, crashed in France on its maiden flight in 1930. Forty-eight passengers and crew lost their lives. In 1937 the Hindenburg burst into flames - the entire disaster caught on camera and described by a distraught reporter. The days of the airship were numbered.

SPORTING CHANCE

In 1939 British racing driver Sir Malcolm Campbell hit the headlines when he captured the world's water-speed record for the third time in 'Bluebird' - all his cars were given the same name. A racing driver who set world speed records both on land and on water, Sir Malcolm established world land-speed records no fewer than nine times. His son Donald went on to set further records, tragically dying in 1967 when his speedboat - also named 'Bluebird' - crashed.

built in 1843 only stood for 46 years; it was dark, dismal, and hated by every person who had to sit in its pews, few of which had a clear view of the pulpit or the altar. The present church replaced it in 1889, and as every Portmuthian who values engineering genius knows, Isambard Kingdom Brunel was christened at St Mary's in the year of his birth, 1806.

Above: The shops may have changed, but even so this is a spot which is instantly recognisable. The Milk Bar in Commercial Road was convenient for travellers, who could grab a sandwich while waiting for their train. At one time Milk Bars were a common sight in virtually every high street. An ideal place to pop in for a quick cup of tea or coffee and a snack, these pleasant and cosy establishments remained popular until the late 50s, when they began to give way to the 'coffee bar'. Today, the City pub offers stronger refreshment near this spot. The University bookshop Chapter and Verse, and Kwik News have replaced these businesses; the old Post Office on the other side of the bridge, is also long gone. Classic car enthusiasts will immediately spot the Morris Minor, interestingly the first all-British car to sell more than one million. Developed by designer Alexander Issigonis, who also gave us the Mini, this tough little car has remained popular and is today attracting quite a following.

Right: The Guildhall, dominating the skyline, is still clad in scaffolding during its rebuilding programme in this view which dates from 1957. If we could see the entire length of the railway bridge we would see that the Ales being advertised were United; we *can* see, however, that the wall beneath the bridge is being taken advantage of as an advertisement hoarding. Here you could check on the forthcoming shows at the Kings Theatre and the Classic Cinema, where at the time 'Helen of Troy' was the 'big picture' and 'A Lawless Street' the supporting film. Those were the days, of course, where you really got your money's worth at the cinema; not only would you see the main film, but the newsreel, a couple of cartoons and a shorter movie. Not that the passers-by were taking much notice of the shows being advertised. Perhaps they were heading for Finlays sweets and tobacco shop to pick up 20 Players, or for Peter's Place, where 'hot meals served all day' would perhaps be an even greater attraction.

These shoppers in London road are spoilt for choice; after topping up their funds at Barclays or the Trustee Savings Bank they could choose a new pair of shoes, pop into Bargain Wallpapers and decide whether pink or blue wallpaper would look best in the bedroom, buzz around Tesco for their groceries, buy the latest Dansette record player in the Civic's showroom - and pop down the road for the latest Rolling Stones LP to play on it. 'His Master's Voice' records are being prominently advertised at the record shop on the corner of Laburnum Grove; at the time of the photograph you could choose between 45s, EPs and LPs. Remember EPs? (These, for the benefit of readers too young to remember, were

Events of the 1930s

MELODY MAKERS
Throughout the 1930s a young American trombonist called Glenn Miller was making his mark in the world of music. By 1939 the Glenn Miller sound was a clear leader in the field; his clean-cut, meticulously executed arrangements of numbers such as 'A String of Pearls' and 'Moonlight Serenade' brought him fame across the world as a big-band leader. During a flight to England from Paris in 1944 Miller's plane disappeared; no wreckage was ever found.

THE WORLD AT LARGE
In India, Gandhi's peaceful protests against British rule were gathering momentum. The Salt Laws were a great bone of contention: forced to buy salt from the British government, thousands of protestors marched to the salt works, intending to take it over in the name of the Indian people. Policemen and guards attacked the marchers, but not one of them fought back. Gandhi, who earned for himself the name 'Mahatma' - Great Soul - was assassinated in 1948.

INVENTION AND TECHNOLOGY
With no driving tests or speed restrictions, 120,000 people were killed on the roads in Britain between the two world wars. In 1934 Percy Shaw invented a safety device destined to become familiar the world over: reflecting roadstuds. In dark or foggy conditions the studs that reflected light from the car's headlights kept traffic on the 'straight and narrow' and must over the years have saved many lives.

extended play, longer than 45 rpm's and not as long as long playing records.) The HMV logo is one of the 20th Century's most well known trademarks. The small dog in their advert was top dog Nipper, whose master, the English artist Francis Barraud, painted him alongside a gramophone he borrowed from the Gramophone Company. The company eventually bought the picture and adopted it as their trademark.

> *Opened in 1937, the Co-op survived the bombs delivered by the Luftwaffe*

We are given an opportunity to take a trip down Memory Lane as a Number 8 Devon Road bus stops at the zebra crossing to allow shoppers to cross Fratton Road. Readers will remember browsing at Portsmouth's large Co-operative department store, and perhaps rounding off your shopping excursion with a meal in the top floor restaurant. Whether you wanted to buy a pair of shoes, a three piece suite or a china tea set, you would find it at the Co-op; remember the pneumatic cash tube that used to whisk your money away and deliver your change and receipt a minute or two later, as if by magic? Opened in 1937, the building survived the bombs delivered by the Luftwaffe and was restored, though it later fell victim to the hungry bulldozer and was replaced by The Bridge Centre shopping mall. The vehicles in the photograph will immediately draw the eye of the enthusiast, from the Escort van, workhorse of the small building firm, to the Wartburg estate car standing at the kerb outside the Co-op. Manufactured behind the Iron Curtain the vehicle - still seen in parts of Germany into the 1990s had a three-cylinder, two-stroke engine which used a petrol and oil mix; its obnoxious exhaust fumes would probably spell immediate MOT failure today.

Wartime

In 1939 Britain's Prime Minister Neville Chamberlain had made his announcement to the waiting people of Britain that '...this country is at war with Germany.' The country rolled up its sleeves and prepared for the inevitable. This war would be different from other wars. This time planes had the ability to fly further and carry a heavier load, and air raids were fully expected. Air raid shelters were obviously going to be needed, and shelters were built on open places across the town.

By the time war was declared an army of volunteers of both sexes had already been recruited to form an Air Raid Protection service. At first ARP personnel were unpaid volunteers but when war broke out in September 1939 they became paid staff. It was their job to patrol specified areas, making sure that no chinks of light broke the blackout restrictions, checking the safety of local residents, being alert for gas attacks, air raids and unexploded bombs. The exceptional work done by Air Raid Wardens in dealing with incendiaries, giving first aid to the injured, helping to rescue victims from their bombed-out properties, clearing away rubble, and a thousand and one other tasks became legendary; during the second world war nearly as many private citizens were killed as troops - and many of them were the gallant ARP wardens.

At the beginning of the war Sir Anthony Eden, Secretary of State for War, appealed in a radio broadcast for men between 17 and 65 to make up a new force, the Local Defence Volunteers, to guard vulnerable points from possible Nazi attack. Within a very short time the first men were putting their names down. At first the new force had to improvise; there were no weapons to spare and men had to rely on sticks, shotguns handed in by local people, and on sheer determination . Weapons and uniforms did not become available for several months.

In July the Local Defence Volunteers was renamed the Home Guard, and by the following year were a force to be reckoned with. Television programmes such as 'Dad's Army' have unfortunately associated the Home Guard with comedy, but in fact they performed much important work. The Guard posted sentries to watch for possible aircraft or parachute landings at likely spots such as disused aerodromes, golf courses on the outskirts of towns, local parks and racecourses. They manned anti-aircraft rocket guns, liaised with other units and with regular troops, set up communications and organised balloon barrages.

Other preparations were hastily made around the town. Place names and other identifying marks were obliterated to confuse the enemy about exactly where they were. Notices went up everywhere giving good advice to citizens on a number of issues. 'Keep Mum - she's not so dumb' warned people to take care what kind of information they passed on, as the person they were speaking to could be an enemy.

Older readers will remember how difficult it was to find certain items in the shops during the war; combs, soap, cosmetics, hairgrips, elastic, buttons, zips - all were virtually impossible to buy as factories that once produced these items had been turned over to war work. Stockings were in short supply, and resourceful women resorted to colouring their legs with gravy browning or with a mixture of sand and water. Beetroot juice was found to be a good substitute for lipstick.

Clothes rationing was introduced in 1941, and everyone had 66 coupons per year. Eleven coupons would buy a dress, and sixteen were needed for a coat. The number of coupons was later reduced to 40 per person. People were required to save material where they could - ladies' hemlines went up considerably, and skirts were not allowed to have lots of pleats. Some found clever ways around the regulations by using materials that were not rationed. Blackout material could be embroidered and made into blouses or skirts, and dyed sugar sacks were turned into curtains.

Above: War had been declared, and every citizen of Britain, young and old, male and female, was called upon to put his or her back into the war effort. Those who did not go into military service of one kind or another worked in factories, dug for victory, gave up their aluminium baths and saucepans, joined organisations and aided in any way they could. These boys were not going to be left out; they might be too young to fight but while there were sandbags to be filled they were going to do their bit to protect their school building. Thousands of sandbags were used during World War II to protect the country and its beautiful civic buildings.

Right: A proud father poses for the camera with his latest arrival. The baby had not arrived from Mars, in fact the 'arrival' was not a baby at all, but an anti-gas attack suit which was compulsory for babies in the United Kingdom during the second world war. An air pump at the side of the suit enabled anxious parents to replenish the supply of air to the precious package inside. It is said that most babies were less than enthusiastic abut the prospect of being encased in the suit - and who could blame them? The picture was taken in 1939. In the event there was never any gas attack on British soil during the course of the second world war.

The Lord Mayor and a group of Air Raid Precautions staff escaped with their lives but little else in the major air raid of 10th January 1941. As showers of incendiaries fell on the Guildhall, fire rapidly spread through the beautiful building. A high explosive bomb followed, scoring a direct hit. The Guildhall, opened by the Prince of Wales (later Edward VII) in 1890, had firmly established itself as an important part of the city's life, and as the tower burned fiercely all the following day the sight was enough to reduce passers-by to tears. There was no saving the building; the interior, with its superb walnut panelling, mosaics, statues and works of art, was completely destroyed and the outer walls were all that remained. It was weeks before the building cooled down sufficiently to allow teams of workers to begin the clearing-up operations - and one pleasant surprise awaited them. As they entered the muniment room below the tower, they found that the historic Corporation plate, part of which dated from the 16th century, the city archives, and the 17th century mace, had been protected from the worst of the heat by the position of the room, and had survived intact.

This page and overleaf: Rows of glassless windows gaze forlornly out across a scene of desolation; damaged frames hang to one side, their shattered glass in poised lethal shards *(below)*. Above, roof timbers lay open to the weather, stripped of their tiles. Was one of these houses the home of the two boys sitting on boxes on the pavement? In a bleak scene of devastation that was all too common in wartime Portsmouth, these lads, aged 10 or 11 and still in short trousers, are the only living thing. Were their toy guns, cowboy outfits and cars among the items lost in the raid? Atterbury's chemist shop at the end of the block has also been badly damaged, and the

large Virol advert, which had been a familiar sight in the neighbourhood for many years, no longer advised passers-by that Virol was 'a wonderful flesh former'. Let it never be said that nutrition was an unimportant issue until the latter half of the 20th century! Virol, for those who have never sampled the delicious stuff, was a malt extract that resembled molasses.

Events of the 1940s

WHAT'S ON?
In wartime Britain few families were without a wireless set. It was the most popular form of entertainment, and programmes such as ITMA, Music While You Work and Workers' Playtime provided the people with an escape from the harsh realities of bombing raids and ration books. In 1946 the BBC introduced the Light Programme, the Home Service and the Third Programme, which gave audiences a wider choice of listening.

GETTING AROUND
October 1948 saw the production of Britain's first new car designs since before the war. The Morris Minor was destined for fame as one of the most popular family cars, while the four-wheel-drive Land Rover answered the need for a British-made off-road vehicle. The country was deeply in the red, however, because of overseas debts incurred during the war. The post-war export drive that followed meant that British drivers had a long wait for their own new car.

SPORTING CHANCE
American World Heavyweight Boxing Champion Joe Louis, who first took the title back in 1937, ruled the world of boxing during the 1930s and 40s, making a name for himself as unbeatable. Time after time he successfully defended his title against all comers, finally retiring in 1948 after fighting an amazing 25 title bouts throughout his boxing career. Louis died in 1981 at the age of 67.

The scene in Dunbar road was heartbreaking, and though teams of workers have moved in to start clearing up, one wonders where you would begin *(right)*. Like ants endeavouring to move an elephant, the wheelbarrows being used on the site seem totally inadequate for the mammoth task ahead. The ladies on the far right, one of whom has sensibly covered her hair with a scarf and tied it into a 'turban', were perhaps residents in the area. If so, their homes, lives and dreams, like those of so many at the time, have turned to dust around their feet. After one devastating attack in 1942 it was at first a case of 'all hands on deck' to help with the clearing away of rubble, dust and bits of plaster, and as soon as possible it was 'business as usual' at the National Provincial Bank in Commercial Road *(above)*. The criminal element would be most unlikely to try to make an entry to the premises during the night; wartime privations drew people together back in the 1940s. Compare this scene with today's banks, with their cctv cameras, panic buttons and glass screens, and we have to admit that the 40s were gentler days indeed.

Between July 1940 and May 1944 Portsmouth endured 67 air raids which wiped out entire areas of the city. Churches, shops, schools, cinemas, pubs and a hospital were destroyed along with more than six and a half thousand private homes. Scenes of total devastation such as this one pictured here in Dunbar Road had become a heartbreaking but familiar sight. A gas cooker from a victim's kitchen lies with its back to the sky; was the family's supper inside it when the bombs began to fall? And on the right, perfectly whole and undamaged, an iron fireplace has been blasted from the chimney breast of someone's bedroom. An Anderson shelter lies still half-buried, not only under garden soil but under debris, which probably came from the owner's home, which is now no more than a heap of rubble. We cannot help but wonder what happened to the family who were more than likely taking shelter here during the raid. Were they among Portsmouth's 930 civilian fatalities of world war two? Many of our more mature readers will still have vivid memories of the air raids, which must have been a terrifying experience. Furniture and other belongings salvaged from the bombed-out homes was taken to a warehouse and put into storage until the owners found somewhere else to live (above). Tables, chairs, beds, washboards, stirrup pumps, the baby's pram and the old chest from the attic - all were labelled with the address from which they were taken and were built into neat stacks until the family called for them. On occasions, of course, there were no survivors of the raid, and the pathetic remnants of people's lives lay here until a relative came along to claim them. Sad times.

Daintily presented scones and jam tarts, pristine table cloths, dainty cups and saucers - even vases of seasonal flowers to bring a touch of life and colour to the table...a far cry from normal daily life on board ship or in the mess (left). This cosy scene was snapped at the Royal Sailors' Rest, a multi-service establishment where every effort was made to give the men a reminder of home. The work was begun by Miss Agnes Weston and her friend and helper Sophia Wintz. A sincere Christian, Agnes was an energetic young woman who spent time visiting the sick, helping the needy, teaching Sunday School and counselling those who desperately needed advice. The Sailors' Rest began, strangely enough, with letters written to a Christian soldier serving overseas. Others asked if she would write to them also, and the work snowballed. Agnes cared deeply for the welfare of such young men who found themselves away from home for long periods of time. Back in port, alcohol was readily available to them, and for many, alcohol abuse signalled the beginning of a downwards slide. In 1874, she and Sophia opened a temperance house, offering hot meals, a bed for the night - and the gospel of Christ. Aggie, as she came to be known among the sailors, lived through World War I to carry on serving. She was never to know of the devastation the second world war brought to the Royal Sailors' Rest, by that time situated on the corner of Commercial Road and Edinburgh Road (above). She died on 23rd October 1918, and was granted the honour of a full naval funeral, so highly was her work regarded. Others picked up the torch, and the refuge continued to be 'home from home' to many after her death - and still continues so today. When the building was destroyed by enemy bombs in October 1941, a mobile Royal Sailors' Rest Canteen was installed, and undeterred, the good work continued. A sharp eye will spot the fact that for security reasons, ships' names have been deleted from these sailors' uniforms.

At leisure

Below: The landing stage at Southsea was not only the place to board one of the many pleasure craft which carried sightseers around the harbour to view the warships, but it also made a superb bathing platform. This scene of fun in the somewhat watery sun was captured in 1938, and though the day looks reasonably pleasant there are still more people sitting around on the landing stage than swimming in the water! The style of swimwear has changed more than a little since then; a few of the men are still sporting all-in-one costumes with shoulder-straps, and although at the time two-piece costumes were beginning to be seen among the ladies, bikinis were undreamed of back then. It was 1946 when the skimpy costumes were created by French designer Louis Reard, and the daring new swimwear that revealed flesh hitherto unseen in public was immediately labelled indecent and immodest....If they could see us now! Swimming caps (usually made of white rubber and with an uncomfortable strap that fastened under the chin), were customary among the ladies, and remained popular until recent years. Today, their use seems to have all but been abandoned - probably because they never did keep out the water anyway!

Long before the days of the artificial wave machine, these children are creating waves of their own. Having a whale of a time in the bathing pool has always been part of summer fun. How many readers can remember those long ago days when their own mums watched from the comfort of a deck chair while they splashed around in this very same pool? It's quite possible that some might recognise themselves in this photograph, which would probably date from some time in the 1930s, and remember that sunny day in their far-off childhood. The bathing pool was a popular feature of the Southsea summer season, and the charge of three-pence included swimming instruction, the use of the nearby playground, and deckchairs for the parents. Beyond the bathing pool, Mum and Dad have a good view of the boating lake. Will this be the family's next port of call? Dad will hopefully be rested by then, and ready to take up the oars for a circuit or two of the lake, with oft-repeated warnings to the kids to 'for goodness' sake, sit still'. Mum, with nothing much to do for a change, can sit back and trail an idle hand in the cool water and enjoy the rare opportunity to have a rest. The bathing pool, along with the boating lake, no longer exist except as treasured memories.

Where shall we sit? That was a question which often cropped up back in 1938, when package tours to Benidorm were unknown and undreamed of. Bewildered sun-seekers looking hopefully around for a few square feet of beach where they can spread out a towel or erect a deck chair were a common sight at Southsea. When the family eventually managed to

find a space Dad was at last able to relax, shade his eyes with a newspaper, and drift off to sleep while Mum read her 'Oracle' and the children headed off towards the sea for a paddle. It's when they wanted to find their way back to Mum and Dad again that the real problems began. Readers who ever, as children, found themselves alone and lost on a

crowded beach will remember how much alike are people dressed in shorts and sitting in deck chairs! After a frantic search, often with floods of tears and perhaps the help of some sympathetic and motherly soul, Mum and Dad would at last be run to earth - and the children greeted with a cry of 'Where have you been? We've been looking everywhere for you.' Oh, the joys of a day by the sea....

Events of the 1940s

HOT OFF THE PRESS
At the end of World War II in 1945 the Allies had their first sight of the unspeakable horrors of the Nazi extermination camps they had only heard of until then. In January, 4,000 emaciated prisoners more dead than alive were liberated by the Russians from Auschwitz in Poland, where three million people, most of them Jews, were murdered. The following year 23 prominent Nazis faced justice at Nuremberg; 12 of them were sentenced to death for crimes against humanity.

THE WORLD AT LARGE
The desert area of Alamogordo in New Mexico was the scene of the first atomic bomb detonation on July 16, 1945. With an explosive power equal to more than 15,000 tons of TNT, the flash could be seen 180 miles away. President Truman judged that the bomb could secure victory over Japan with far less loss of US lives than a conventional invasion, and on 6th August the first of the new weapons was dropped on Hiroshima. Around 80,000 people died.

ROYAL WATCH
By the end of World War II, the 19-year-old Princess Elizabeth and her distant cousin Lieutenant Philip Mountbatten RN were already in love. The King and Queen approved of Elizabeth's choice of husband, though they realised that she was rather young and had not mixed with many other young men. The engagement announcement was postponed until the Princess had spent four months on tour in Africa. The couple's wedding on 20th November 1947 was a glittering occasion - the first royal pageantry since before the war.

How many readers remember swimming at Hilsea Lido? The weather had to be very warm before the average person was brave enough to go swimming at the Lido, but there were always some intrepid souls who would defy those cooler days and don their swimming costumes. On the day that this marvellous view was captured, however, there were no such worries. The 32-foot tall top board of the diving tower was ideal for high diving displays, and frozen in time for ever by the camera, a descending diver is caught in a superb pose. Opened in 1936 at a cost of £40,000, the cascades at each end of the 220-foot long open air pool aerated the water, while an up-to-date method of filtration effected a change of water every six hours. Most age groups were catered for at the Lido, from the children's 2ft 6ins depth to the 15ft needed by divers.

Above: A magnet for all youngsters, whether they lived locally or were spending their fortnight's holiday in Southsea - the miniature railway on Southsea Common. The mini railway, which had real engines and tenders with their own station, tunnel and signals, drew a host of fathers, who no doubt envied the fortunate man who was lucky enough to have landed the job of driving this little beauty. Any one of them would no doubt have been only too willing to part with cash from their own pockets for the privilege of driving the engine, which ran on a nine and a half inch gauge track, on its regular excursions around the Common. It was 1929 when a large area was set aside by the council as a children's park. The railway, a boating lake, paddling pool, sandpit and swings, were a huge success, aided without a doubt by the 1929 guide book issued by the council, which included a full-colour, 40-inch panorama of Portsmouth painted by the well-known marine artist William Wyllie. An amazing total of 33,000 guide books were issued that year, many of them being sent across the world. How many of our readers still have a copy tucked away in a box in the loft?

Top: If you could afford to enjoy the better things in life and did not set too much store on positioning yourself a few feet from the sea, then a sun hut was the ideal way to avoid the crowded Southsea beach. The huts, situated between the South Parade Pier and Eastney, were very popular and became a home from home, both for long-term visitors and residents who loved to spend the summer weekends relaxing out of doors. Pictured outside their huts in 1938, these families are enjoying the warm sunshine, some relaxing with a good book and others simply topping up their tan. Our more mature lady readers will remember wearing swimming costumes just like these, made from a silk-like material (rayon perhaps?) ruched with fine elastic and not a cleavage in sight! They must have been regarded as attractive at the time, though we may look back now and wonder why! The sun huts were well equipped with electric kettles and a power point, a locker, a drop-down table, and two deck chairs. Many would spend the entire day in their huts, even installing their primus stoves there so that they could make a hot meal! Rental on a sun hut for the summer months would have set you back exactly £2.

Events of the 1940s

MELODY MAKERS
The songs of radio personalities such as Bing Crosby and Vera Lynn were whistled, sung and hummed everywhere during the 1940s. The 'forces' sweetheart' brought hope to war-torn Britain with 'When the Lights go on Again', while the popular crooner's 'White Christmas' is still played around Christmas time even today. Who can forget songs like 'People Will Say we're in Love', 'Don't Fence Me In', 'Zip-a-dee-doo-dah', and 'Riders in the Sky'?

INVENTION AND TECHNOLOGY
Inspired by quick-drying printers' ink, in 1945 Hungarian journalist Laszlo Biro developed a ballpoint pen which released viscous ink from its own reservoir as the writer moved the pen across the page. An American inventor was working on a similar idea at the same time, but it was Biro's name that stuck. A few years later Baron Bich developed a low cost version of the pen, and the 'Bic' ballpoint went on sale in France in 1953.

SCIENCE AND DISCOVERY
In 1943 Ukrainian-born biochemist Selman Abraham Waksman made a significant discovery. While studying organisms found in soil he discovered an antibiotic (a name Waksman himself coined) which was later found to be the very first effective treatment for tuberculosis. A major killer for thousands of years, even the writings of the ancient Egyptians contain stories of people suffering from tuberculosis. Waksman's development of streptomycin brought him the 1952 Nobel Prize for Medicine.

Those who revel in the touch of the sun on their faces have claimed their own few yards of space on the beach at Southsea, quite a feat in pre-war Britain, when foreign holidays were the province of the affluent and the average family headed here from all over the British Isles in search of sun and sea, if not Sangria! The tide was out on this hot summer's day back in 1938, giving the holidaymakers a wide expanse of beach to spread out on.

Even so, it was rather crowded - a definite bonus for the cafe serving tea, coffee and sandwiches, possibly on trays which could be taken on to the beach. Though the threat of war hung over the country when this view was captured, no shadow of gloom hangs over the happy scene. Sunshine and blue skies were vital ingredients of a day spent on the beach, though for those less than perfect days the nearby pier with its multitude of attractions presented the visitor with plenty of alternatives. A similar view can be had from the same spot today; a cafeteria still stands on the same spot, though a modern block of flats has been built next to the Ocean Hotel.

The King's Theatre holds a very special place in the affections of all Portmuthians, a mixture of Tommy Trinder, 'Swan Lake', and 'Whistle Down the Wind' weaving themselves into your memories across the years. Remember the pantomimes you saw there as children? Interactive or what! Boos and hisses. Cinderella and Buttons; the fairy godmother; the ugly sisters and, of course, the prince, complete with shapely legs and high heels. The times you shouted 'He's behind you!' and responded to the inevitable 'Oh no he isn't' with 'Oh yes he is!' Great stuff. The 2,172-seat King's Theatre opened in September 1907, and as films grew in popularity they were shown during the afternoons, though evenings were still dedicated to live music hall. The first talkie was shown in 1931, and for a time the facility was dedicated to films. Fortunately for us, the King's reverted to theatre, and still remains one of Southsea's major attractions. The beautiful building came through the war unscathed, and remained open to delight audiences into the 21st century with ballet, musicals, plays and traditional pantomime. Bernard Dupont's Big Show of Stars - billed as 'Southsea's great star-studded review' - was the twice-nightly show at the time of this photograph, with big names Tommy Trinder and Anne Shelton as the star attractions.

Below: The year was 1944, and the Odeon in North End were advertising the following week's show in a heap big way - far more so than the film which was actually being screened at the time. The current film happened to be 'The Uninvited', a ghostly tale shot in black and white that same year, and which attracted rave reviews ('It will hold audiences glued to their seats' - Variety). Perhaps the supporting film, 'Winefields around the World', was rather less able to pull in the punters in their hundreds.... An early example of Technicolor (1943), 'Melody Inn' unfortunately failed - according to the reviewers of the day - to live up to expectations. The billboard promises audiences 'a riot of laughs' though the film was judged to have neither wit nor style. Damning words. 'Riding High' was the US title, and Dorothy Lamour and Dick Powell were the main protagonists. Film buffs will no doubt remember that the plot of the film centres around a burlesque queen who returns to her home in Arizona, where to help out local ranchers she agrees to stage a performance. Milt Britton and his band provided 'plenty hep songs', while Dorothy Lamour was as alluring as she could be while wearing a grass skirt.

Bottom: The tearjerker 'Johnny Belinda' was being screened at the Theatre Royal when this scene was caught on camera. Made in black and white in 1948, the subject of the film was quite daring for its time; a young deaf mute girl, played by Jane Wyman, is raped and subsequently gives birth to a child. Suspicion falls upon the sympathetic local doctor - and the whole affair causes an uproar in a remote fishing community. In spite of its controversial content, the film attracted good reviews and made a big star of Jane Wyman. When the building suffered extensive damage during a bombing raid in world war two, many had believed the well-loved old theatre to be beyond repair. Extensive reconstruction gave new life to the Prince's Theatre, and to Portsmouth's credit the beautiful building has been preserved and continues to delight audiences today.

Events of the 1940s

WHAT'S ON?
In wartime Britain few families were without a wireless set. It was the most popular form of entertainment, and programmes such as ITMA, Music While You Work and Workers' Playtime provided the people with an escape from the harsh realities of bombing raids and ration books. In 1946 the BBC introduced the Light Programme, the Home Service and the Third Programme, which gave audiences a wider choice of listening.

GETTING AROUND
October 1948 saw the production of Britain's first new car designs since before the war. The Morris Minor was destined for fame as one of the most popular family cars, while the four-wheel-drive Land Rover answered the need for a British-made off-road vehicle. The country was deeply in the red, however, because of overseas debts incurred during the war. The post-war export drive that followed meant that British drivers had a long wait for their own new car.

SPORTING CHANCE
American World Heavyweight Boxing Champion Joe Louis, who first took the title back in 1937, ruled the world of boxing during the 1930s and 40s, making a name for himself as unbeatable. Time after time he successfully defended his title against all comers, finally retiring in 1948 after fighting an amazing 25 title bouts throughout his boxing career. Louis died in 1981 at the age of 67.

This page and overleaf: Whether you are looking for the thrills of the fairground, a little flutter on the slot machines, a sea trip, or the freedom of the beach, Southsea has long possessed every conceivable entertainment for that long looked-for two-week holiday by the sea.

The funfair at Clarence Pier had an atmosphere of its very own that had to be experienced to be appreciated. *(above)* The whirr and hum of the rides, the loud beat of the music, several different tunes fighting with each other for attention, the shouts of the man who bravely volunteered to guess your weight, the squeals of the girls as they rose to the top of the big wheel. And the food! The shocking pink candy floss that was sold from booths and was spun around a stick while you

waited, the toffee apples, dark red and shining as if they had been varnished, the paper bags of crunchy brandy snap and the ice cream, in tubs, cornets or wafers. A more substantial meal was to be had nearby in the cafes, snack bars and fish and chip restaurants along the esplanade, with tea, coffee, and fizzy pop by the gallon *(above)*. And if something a little stronger was more to your taste, the Seahorse bar was a convenient watering hole. Clarence Pier, constructed in 1861, catered largely

for the Isle of Wight steamer trade, and particularly on holiday weekends it became a very lively attraction. In more recent years the hovercraft terminal, constructed near the pier, badly affected the boat trips. By the late 1950s many more families owned a car, though the car park on the left still appears to have spaces available. Clearly, a trolley bus service ran to the esplanade for the convenience of the majority of people, who travelled by public transport.

Left: A little dog pauses for thought in the middle of Festing Road, though the distinct lack of traffic ensures that he will live to bark another day. On one of the busy main routes to the sea front, the little dog would not last long today! Is the young girl - with a toddler tucked away out of sight behind her - his owner, we wonder? Today the teenager would not be seen wearing short socks and sensible shoes, but back in the 40s and 50s children enjoyed their childhood and remained children far longer than do the worldly-wise kids of today. Pleasant gardens have replaced the luxurious Southsea Odeon, where 'Cheers for Miss Bishop' (events in the life of a small town schoolmistress, described as 'sentimental hokum') was playing at the time of the photograph. Built in 1937, the ultra-modern cinema was the last word in comfort. Cinema-going was a favourite entertainment at the time, and remained so throughout the war years and into the 1950s. Sadly, the growing popularity of television spelled the beginning of the end for many cinemas; the Odeon managed to continue until 1985, but eventually succumbed and was demolished.

Above: 'You get the best of both mediums at the Victoria Hall,' declared the publicity statement for the Victoria Hall back in 1929, when talking pictures came to Portsmouth's very first cinema. The old silent films, after all, could not be replaced overnight, and for some time the Victoria Hall orchestra continued to supply music appropriate to the drama, the excitement or the pathos of those wonderful old films. Photographed in 1960 in its final days of life, the Victoria cinema had already shown its last film - 'Expresso Bongo' - and was awaiting demolition. The Victoria was not only Portsmouth's oldest cinema but could also claim to be one of the very first in Britain. The 'films' put on in 1896 however were little more than moving photographs of dancers and boxers strutting their respective stuff, but the novelty value was there at the cost of 6d for the half hour show. It was 1908 when the hall became a full time cinema, though a couple of disastrous fires, fed by the highly inflammable film in the projection room, almost put paid to the concern. In 1950 the Deputy Lord Mayor cut a celebration cake on the occasion of the Victoria Cinema's Golden Jubilee - though paying homage to the building's history did nothing to stay the planners' red pen. A university department today stands in its place.

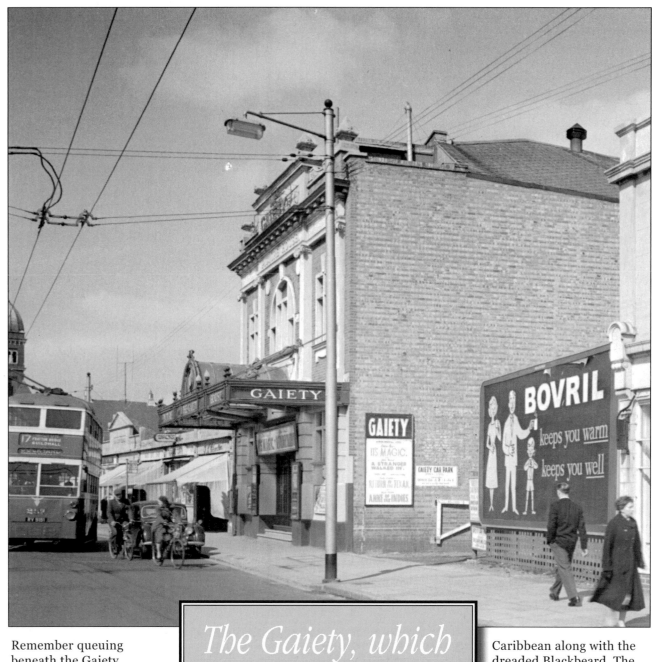

The Gaiety, which opened in February 1924, showed its last film in 1959

Remember queuing beneath the Gaiety cinema's ornate canopy to watch Judy Garland, Kirk Douglas, Cary Grant - or even Roy Rogers and his four-legged friend Trigger? You might, of course, equally well remember queuing in Henley Road, as the Gaiety was unusual in possessing two box offices.... 'It's Magic' was showing at the time of the photograph, a musical which launched Doris Day and her golden voice on the road to stardom. Billed as a coming attraction was 'Anne of the Indies' - nothing to do with L M Montgomery's enchanting 'Anne' books. This was about the lady pirate Anne Bonney, buckling her charming swash in the Caribbean along with the dreaded Blackbeard. The Gaiety, opened in February 1924, was to show its last film in 1959 - a year after this photograph.

Old adverts are as much a part of nostalgia as the long-gone buildings, and lovers of trivia might like to know that Bovril was first sold as Johnston's Fluid Beef in 1874. Within a few years their slogans, not without a touch of humour ('I hear they want more!' says one nervous bull to another), had made Bovril into a household name. The catchphrase 'Bovril prevents that sinking feeling' was designed before World War I but was withheld at the time as a mark of respect for the families of those lost on the 'Titanic'.

This page: Developing that lightning instinct involves training indoors as well as on the pitch, and during a session in the gym a photographer catches the squad and their coach in his viewfinder *(bottom)*. The scene dates from the 1960s - not the greatest time for Pompey, who had suffered nine humiliating defeats in a row in the 1962 season. After thrashing Leeds 3-0 in April things began to look up, and further wins saved the club from relegation. As the season finished, Pompey were 16th in the second division. That summer Smith signed winger John McClelland from QPR, full back Roy Lunniss from Crystal Palace, and later, Brian Lewis from the same club. The 1963-64 season began on an upbeat note with a 2-0 victory at Manchester City, though the club continued to struggle. Pompey owed much to top-shot Ron Saunders (is this he, standing, on the far left of the photograph taken in August 1964? *Below left)*, who scored his first league hat-trick in October as Fratton hosted Newcastle - a game that ended in a 5-2 win. Saunders kept the goals flowing - which made Smith's decision to accept Watford's £15,000 offer for Saunders all the more inexplicable. As the season drew to a close, Pompey fought their way back to 16th place in the league.

It's more than 100 years since Portsmouth FC was formed, and by the 1930s things began to buzz, backed by the appointment of players such as Jimmy Guthrie, Bert Barlow and Jock Anderson. The club's greatest hour came in 1939 as the clouds of war hung low over Britain. It was 29th April when, in a 4-1 victory over Wolverhampton Wanderers, Pompey lifted the FA Cup at Wembley. The strains of 'Who's afraid of the big, bad Wolf' accompanied the team as they took the cup home in triumph, mobbed by thousands of supporters. It was time to let the champagne corks pop!

Events of the 1950s

WHAT'S ON?

Television hit Britain in a big way during the 1950s. Older readers will surely remember 'Double Your Money, Dixon of Dock Green and 'Dragnet' (whose characters' names were changed 'to protect the innocent'). Commercial television was introduced on 22nd September 1955, and Gibbs SR toothpaste were drawn out of the hat to become the first advert to be shown. Many believed adverts to be vulgar, however, and audiences were far less than had been hoped for.

GETTING AROUND

The year 1959 saw the development of the world's first practical air-cushion vehicle - better known to us as the hovercraft. The earliest model was only able to travel at slow speeds over very calm water and was unable to carry more than three passengers. The faster and smoother alternative to the sea ferry quickly caught on, and by the 1970s a 170-ton car-carrying hovercraft service had been introduced across the English Channel.

SPORTING CHANCE

The four-minute mile had remained the record since 1945, and had become regarded as virtually unbreakable. On 6th May 1954, however, Oxford University student Roger Bannister literally ran away with the record, accomplishing the seemingly impossible in three minutes 59.4 seconds. Bannister collapsed at the end of his last amazing lap, even temporarily losing his vision. By the end of the day, however, he had recovered sufficiently to celebrate his achievement in a London night club!

It was back in the mid 1920s when various attractions were installed on Southsea Common to pull in the tourists. As well as children's entertainment of various kinds, an all-out effort was made by the council to accommodate the sporting visitor. The sports of football, lacrosse, bowling and putting were catered for - as, of course, was tennis.

Hard courts were built as well as grass, and Southsea became well known for the quality of its courts and its potential as a venue for big matches. The men's doubles, pictured in Southsea in 1952, has pulled in a large crowd of spectators to follow the progress of the players. The courts are of course still very much in use today, and are a venue for the All England County Championships. In June, just before Wimbledon, many of the big tennis stars can be seen here. Southsea one week, Wimbledon the next.... Game, set and match to good old Southsea!

Events & occasions

Below: The number of spectators around the bowling green informs us that this was an important match. Some of the luckier ones have managed to secure a deck chair or a bench, though others were quite prepared to stand. Though the spectators in the foreground might appear on the surface to be quite relaxed, the rapt attention nevertheless betrays an atmosphere of tension as a high point in the match is reached.

When the War Department sold Southsea Common to Portsmouth Council in 1922, they spent £60,000 on providing residents and holidaymakers with a wide variety of sporting facilities and children's playgrounds. Along with a football pitch, tennis courts, a putting green and even a lacrosse pitch, the area was provided with no fewer than seven bowling greens, and the various clubs held out a warm welcome to visitors. Southsea's fine greens established themselves as an important venue for big competitions, and coachloads of bowlers still descend on Southsea today.

Guy Fawkes, eat your heart out! This marvellous fireworks display - a sight to rival the best that any 5th November celebrations had to offer - would have formed a fitting finale for the 1953 Tattoo. Held in Fratton Park football stadium, the Tattoo (literally, an evening bugle call that summoned soldiers to their quarters) was an event that drew crowds of thousands. Contests between different sections of the military, such as field gun trials, would have formed an important part of the show, and displays of their particular skills and specialities kept the entire audience enthralled. And so to the fireworks display. The glowing, shooting colours of the Roman candles, the whizz of a myriad rockets, the crackles and bangs and the shooting stars which lit up the upturned faces in the crowd and called forth oohs and ahs from hundreds of throats, and the distinctive smell of smoke that hung in the air. Pure magic - and all in all, a perfect day.

Navy Days had been going for just ten years when this busy scene was captured in August 1938. In the background, vast crowds are waiting to be admitted to the Dockyard. How many readers were in the queue on this August Bank Holiday? And did you pop into the Keppel's Head to quench your thirst before or after your visit? Known locally as 'The Nut' (why?), the pub belonged to Spicers brewery in the late 19th century. Navy Days was established to aid naval charities, and the popular event has been doing so very successfully ever since. Warships

and submarines would have taken a prominent place in 1938, 13 months before Britain declared war on Nazi Germany, and ARP displays, poisonous gas demonstrations and perhaps torpedo and depth charge firing could well have formed part of the day's attractions.

In the foreground, a steady flow of people, dressed for the warm summer weather, make their way along the concourse towards Portsmouth Harbour railway station. The station is still very much in use today, especially by travellers meeting the Isle of Wight ferry.

Flags fly high over the Southsea Show in 1957, and the huge crowd of punters browsing among the booths and marquees shows us exactly how popular the annual event had become. In the background, something is happening in the show ring, though we unfortunately can't make out whether this is the judging of prize animals or a dog obedience contest! While a few have seen all they want to see at the show, a queue of people are still waiting at the gate on their way in. The sign to the left reveals a few of the attractions of the day: topping the bill was the Southsea Floral Queen contest, and 20 nervous girls were waiting to be judged on their looks and dress, their hearts no doubt beating very fast. The display of '100 years of fashion in millinery' would have been very popular among the ladies, while the

advertised military band was a pull for all the family.

Some fine cars await their owners in the car park: the A35 van on the left was the choice of work-pony with many small firms; a good old Morris Oxford stands alongside it. Not far away is a Triumph Mayflower, distinguished by its somewhat angular lines, while in the right foreground is a Rover 75. Note the little Austin 7 further back, some driver's treasured possession for many years!

Events of the 1950s

HOT OFF THE PRESS
The 1950s seemed to be the heyday of spies, and in 1951 the activities of Guy Burgess and Donald Maclean caused a sensation in the country. Both had occupied prominent positions in the Foreign Office, while Burgess had also been a member of MI-6. Recruited by the Russians while at Cambridge University in the 1930s, the traitors provided the Soviets with a huge amount of valuable information. They disappeared in 1951, surfacing in Moscow five years later.

THE WORLD AT LARGE
Plans to develop the economies of member states into one common market came to fruition on 1st January 1958, when the EEC came into operation. The original members were France, Belgium, Luxembourg, The Netherlands, Italy, and West Germany. The Community became highly successful, achieving increased trade and prosperity across Western Europe while at the same time alleviating fear of war which lingered on after the end of World War II. Britain became a member in 1973.

SCIENCE AND DISCOVERY
DNA (deoxyribonucleic acid) was first defined as long ago as 1953, and the effects have been far-reaching. The key discovery was developed over the following years and today DNA fingerprinting has become an accepted part of life. Genetic diseases such as hemophilia and cystic fibrosis have been identified. Criminals are continually detected and brought to justice. Biological drugs have been developed. More controversially, drought and disease-resistant plants have been engineered - and Dolly the sheep has been produced.

Twenty pretty girls parade their charms for the judges, and twenty hearts must have been beating nineteen to the dozen as they waited nervously to hear the judges' decision *(above)*. The Floral Queen contest was a popular part of the Southsea Show, and these charming scenes were snapped in August 1957. The dresses of the contestants reflect the fashion of the day, when narrow waists and mid calf length, widely flared skirts were the 'in thing', together with the short, soft perm and Louis heels. Remember paper nylon underskirts? And those frothy net ones? Lady readers who were in their teens and twenties during the 1950s certainly will. Immensely feminine, the crisp petticoats transformed a loosely hanging skirt into a mini 'crinoline' that rustled seductively as they walked. And perhaps our male readers will remember with nostalgia those occasional tantalising glimpses of foaming petticoat! Note also that many of these girls are wearing gloves, at the time the essential accessory to the well-dressed young lady's outfit. Crowned that day as the Southsea Show Floral Queen was the

tall and willowy Number 19, pictured here with the runners-up *(right)*. On her left is Number 11 - a definite wearer of net underskirts - though the number of the other runner up is not known. What a pity that we have not been able to find out their names; perhaps some lady reader will recognise herself among this bevy of beauties!

The feminine face and form was rated highly in Southsea at the time. Regular bathing beauty contests were held on South Parade Pier, with attractive prizes for the lucky winners. This kind of competition was to eventually find itself a victim of 'political incorrectness' as the women's libbers symbolically burnt their bras and declared beauty contests to be demeaning to women. Interestingly, towards the end of the 1990s the idea of the beauty contest once more began to gain popularity, and in places where organisers were brave enough to revive them, the competitions were as much looked forward to by the gorgeous girls hoping for recognition as by holiday-makers who possessed an appreciative eye for the ladies.

No, this warship pictured in Guildhall Square had not lost her way and sailed into the city centre on a particularly high tide. The huge wood and plaster model, HMS Coronation, was built over the tram shelter and formed part of the Coronation Review, held when George VI was crowned in 1937 *(inset)*. After dark, the illuminated ship was a wonderful sight. The marvellous spectacle of a Naval Review will be well remembered by our more mature readers. Younger ones, however, have yet to experience the thrill of seeing for themselves the fleet of ships assembled at Spithead, as the last Review was held to commemorate the Queen's Silver Jubilee in June 1977.

When Georve V died in 1936, his eldest son Edward came to the throne, and King Edward VIII's coronation was planned for 12th May 1937. As we all know, The corona-

tion celebrations that were held did not go according to the original plan. In the event the monarch being crowned was not Edward VIII, who Britain had expected to reign after the death of King George V, but his younger brother. Albert, Duke of York, had been hurled unexpectedly into the kingship he had not been trained for when his older brother Edward VIII, who had been king for a mere 325 days, renounced the throne on 10 December 1936 for American divorcee Wallis Simpson, 'the woman I love.' It was therefore King George VI who reviewed the fleet at Spithead in 1937. With him was Queen Elizabeth and their two pretty daughters, Elizabeth (our present Queen) and Margaret Rose. In spite of the fact that the threat of war was already looming on the horizon, the German warship 'Admiral Graf Spee' - destined to be

Graf Spee' - destined to be pursued across the Atlantic, trapped in Montevideo Harbour and subsequently scuttled - was one of the 18 foreign ships present at the Coronation Review.

Though umbrellas and hats were the order of the day, the steadily pouring rain failed to put a damper on the occasion, and hundreds of feet, no doubt, were tapping as the Band of the Royal Marines, distinguished by their pith helmets, played stirring marches *(main picture)*. Many of the Royal Navy's G, H and I class warships and new submarines were at the Review, including the battle cruiser Repulse, which had just undergone a refit. It was an encouraging sight to those who realised that it was simply a matter of time before Britain and Germany were at war. The King and Queen, aboard the royal yacht Victoria and Albert, passed through the lines, a resounding 'three cheers' ringing out from every vessel as the royal party passed. An impressive fly-past by aircraft of the Fleet Air Arm made a fitting finale to the day's events.

Events of the 1950s

MELODY MAKERS
Few teenage girls could resist the blatant sex-appeal of 'Elvis the Pelvis', though their parents were scandalised at the moody Presley's provocatively gyrating hips. The singer took America and Britain by storm with such hits as 'Jailhouse Rock', 'All Shook Up' and 'Blue Suede Shoes'. The rhythms of Bill Haley and his Comets, Buddy Holly and Chuck Berry turned the 1950s into the Rock 'n' Roll years.

INVENTION AND TECHNOLOGY
Until the late 1950s you did not carry radios around with you. Radios were listened to at home, plugged into a mains socket in every average sitting room. Japan was in the forefront of electronic developments even then, and in 1957 the Japanese company Sony introduced the world's very first all-transistor radio - an item of new technology that was small enough to fit into your pocket. The major consumer product caught on fast - particularly with teenage listeners.

ROYAL WATCH
King George VI's health had been causing problems since 1948, when he developed thrombosis. In 1951 the King - always a heavy smoker - became ill again, and was eventually found to be suffering from lung cancer. His left lung was removed in September of 1951. In January 1952 he waved Princess Elizabeth and Prince Philip off on their tour of Africa; they were never to see him again. The King died in the early hours of 6th February 1952.

Below: Smartly turned out for inspection by Brigadier Moss on October 28th 1960, these well-trained soldiers, members of the Royal Army Ordnance Corps at Hilsea Barrack, stand stiffly to attention. Was this their passing out parade? Many will readers will remember the 'spit and polish' that was involved in preparing for such an event. The inspection took place just a month before the last National Servicemen to receive enlistment notices joined their units. Interestingly, a total of 5,300,000 people were called up under the National Service Acts between 1939 and 1960 - and in subsequent years there were still those who held rigidly to the opinion that it should never have been stopped, asserting that army discipline was the best cure for juvenile delinquency. By the end of the decade, Hilsea Barracks itself had ceased to exist and was eventually replaced by a housing estate.

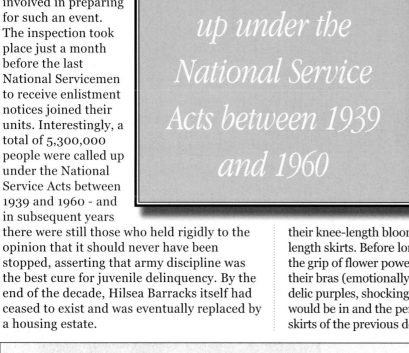

> *A total of 5,300,000 people were called up under the National Service Acts between 1939 and 1960*

Right: Applauded by the audience, a fashion model of 1961 shows off the latest thing in party frocks. South Parade Pier was a regular venue for the fashion shows, which were popular especially among lady visitors, though a number of men can be seen among the audience. The influence of the styles of the previous decade can still be detected in the model's wide skirt, supported by its layers of net underskirt. By the end of the 1960s, however, fashions would have changed beyond recognition as hemlines rose to an all-time high with the invention of tights, scandalising the elderly ladies in this audience who would remain hooked on their knee-length bloomers below mid-calf-length skirts. Before long the country would be in the grip of flower power, girls would have burnt their bras (emotionally if not actually), psyche-delic purples, shocking pinks and brash yellows would be in and the permed hair and flowing skirts of the previous decade most definitely out.

Events of the 1960s

WHAT'S ON?

Television comedy came into its own in the 1960s, and many of the shows that were favourites then went on to become classics. 'On the Buses', 'Steptoe and Son', 'Till Death Us Do Part' and 'The Army Game' kept audiences laughing, while the incredible talents of Morecambe and Wise, the wit of Des O'Connor - often the butt of the duo's jokes - and the antics of Benny Hill established them for ever in the nation's affections.

GETTING AROUND

The 2nd March 1969 was a landmark in the history of aviation. The Anglo-French supersonic airliner Concorde took off for the first time from Toulouse in France. Concorde, which can cruise at almost twice the speed of sound, was designed to fly from London to New York in an incredible three hours twenty minutes. The event took place just weeks after the Boeing 747, which can carry 500 passengers to Concorde's modest 100, made its first flight.

SPORTING CHANCE

Wembley Stadium saw scenes of jubilation when on 30th July 1966 England beat West Germany 4-2 in the World Cup. The match, played in a mixture of sunshine and showers, had been a nailbiting experience for players and spectators alike from the very beginning when Germany scored only thirteen minutes into the game. It was Geoff Hurst's two dramatic goals scored in extra time that secured the victory and lifted the cup for England - at last.

Plants in pots, flower displays, framed pictures, frilly lampshades and much more besides were on offer at the St Matthew's church bazaar. Church members have turned out in force to support the fund raising event, and the vicar too can be spotted in the background, doing a bit of mingling. The Young Wives have their own stall, and we have to hope that the items on sale there found approval under the scrutiny of

the critical eyes of the much older wives. Being a church bazaar, where those attending could be expected to be honest and above board, the lady on the left carrying a shopping basket should find her purchases all present and correct when she leaves for home. The photograph dates from October 1957, and generally speaking those were altogether more honest times. Open-topped shopping baskets were abandoned with the escalating levels of crime in general and shoplifting in particular. Bazaars, along with jumble sales, concerts, bring and buy sales and socials have long been a traditional way for churches around the country to replace their roof or buy a new organ.

It's 'eyes right' for some and 'eyes elsewhere' for others in this scouts' march past in Copnor Road. It was the St George's Day Parade of 1958, and it's quite possible that some of our readers will be among this very smart line of lads and will remember just how great an influence the movement had on their lives. From the very beginning of the scouting movement in the early years of the 20th century, leaders placed great emphasis on personal integrity, and before they were accepted as a scout each of these young boys would have had to promise to do their duty to God and to their country, to help other people, and to obey the Scout law.

Signalling, rope-knotting, mapping, first aid and other skills needed in camping and similar outdoor activities designed to develop self-reliance were part and parcel of scout meetings, and proved to be popular with youngsters. The movement was formed in Poole in 1908, following the publication of Sir Robert Baden-Powell's book 'Scouting for Boys'. The book had been intended for use by existing youth organisations, but it proved to be the beginning of a new, exciting and very popular one.

Below: With no time to stop for luncheon, tea, or even a quick cup of coffee at the Swiss Cafe in Edinburgh Road, the first priority of these dockyard workers, pictured on a wet day in 1958, is to get home at the end of another long day. A hot meal will no doubt be waiting for them, and after that they could look forward to a couple of hours with their mates in the 'Dog and Duck'. If they were the type to enjoy the fireside rather than the tap room, it would be pipe and slippers time, with 'Criss Cross Quiz', 'Take Your Pick' or perhaps 'Emergency Ward Ten' to watch on telly. The sight of literally thousands of workers cycling to and from the Dockyard has long been a familiar one at the beginning and end of every working day. So many men, with so many different skills, from clerks to electrical engineers. Though the Dockyard is no longer what it was in its heyday, it is still very active, repairing and refitting ships and providing shelter and supplies for foreign warships from across the world. Many of the Royal Navy's most modern warships still use Portsmouth as a home base.

A publicity stunt with a difference - these army cadets have been drafted in as part of an advertising campaign to push Tony's Crisps. With the historic HMS Victory in the background, the lads appear to be enjoying their bags of crisps, which seem to have descended into obscurity.

No such tasty fare was available to Victory's crew at the beginning of the 19th century. Their carbohydrates were obtained from a daily supply of one and a quarter pounds of bread or biscuit - which sounds fine until we imagine the same bread and biscuit - and its wriggling

inhabitants - as the voyage progressed week by week. It is said that the men waited until the lights were put out before they ventured to eat it; the old maxim that starts off 'what the eye doesn't see' definitely held true! HMS Victory is arguably the world's most famous ship, and a constant flow of visitors still queue to view the spot where Nelson fell at Trafalgar, and the very place where the famous hero died. The youngest schoolboy or girl in Portsmouth will know by heart his stirring signal: 'England expects that every man will do his duty.'

Events of the 1960s

HOT OFF THE PRESS

Barbed wire, concrete blocks and a wide no-man's-land divided East from West when a reinforced wall was built right across the city of Berlin in 1961. Many East Germans escaped to the West at the eleventh hour, taking with them only the possessions they could carry. The Berlin Wall divided the city - and hundreds of family members and friends - for 28 years until the collapse of Communist rule across Eastern Europe. Who can ever forget those scenes in 1989, when ordinary people themselves began to physically tear down the hated wall?

THE WORLD AT LARGE

'One giant leap for mankind' was taken on 20th July 1969, when Neil Armstrong made history as the first man to set foot on the moon. During the mission he and fellow-astronaut 'Buzz' Aldrin collected rock and soil samples, conducted scientific experiments - and had a lot of fun jumping around in the one-sixth gravity. Twenty-one hours and thirty-seven minutes after their landing they took off again in their lunar module 'Eagle' to rejoin Apollo II which was orbiting above them, proudly leaving the American flag on the Moon's surface.

ROYAL WATCH

Princess Margaret's announcement in 1960 that she was to wed photographer Antony Armstrong-Jones (later Lord Snowdon) brought sighs of relief from her immediate family. Just five years earlier the people of Britain had sympathised as the princess bowed to public and private pressure, ending her relationship with Peter Townsend, Prince Philip's former equerry. The Church (and the Queen, as its Head) frowned on the liaison as Townsend was divorced. Her marriage to Lord Snowdon itself ended in 1978.

When Princess Margaret made a visit to Portsmouth on 26th June 1952, large crowds of enthusiastic royal watchers lined the streets to wave a greeting as she passed by in her smart Daimler limousine. The 1950s were difficult years for the Queen's sister. She had long played an important part in the royal round of official openings, charity events, laying of foundations stones and official tree plantings, and while outwardly

glamorous her life was nevertheless monotonous. Three years hence, the Princess was to end her ill-starred romance with Group Captain Peter Townsend. The couple fell deeply in love and hoped to be allowed to marry. But Townsend, a distinguished fighter pilot, had been married before and had two children. The Princess was reminded of the scandal surrounding her uncle, Edward VIII, when he forfeited his throne to marry divorcee Wallis Simpson - and she chose duty rather than her own happiness. In 1960 she married photographer Antony Armstrong Jones - a marriage which itself was sadly destined to end in divorce in 1978.

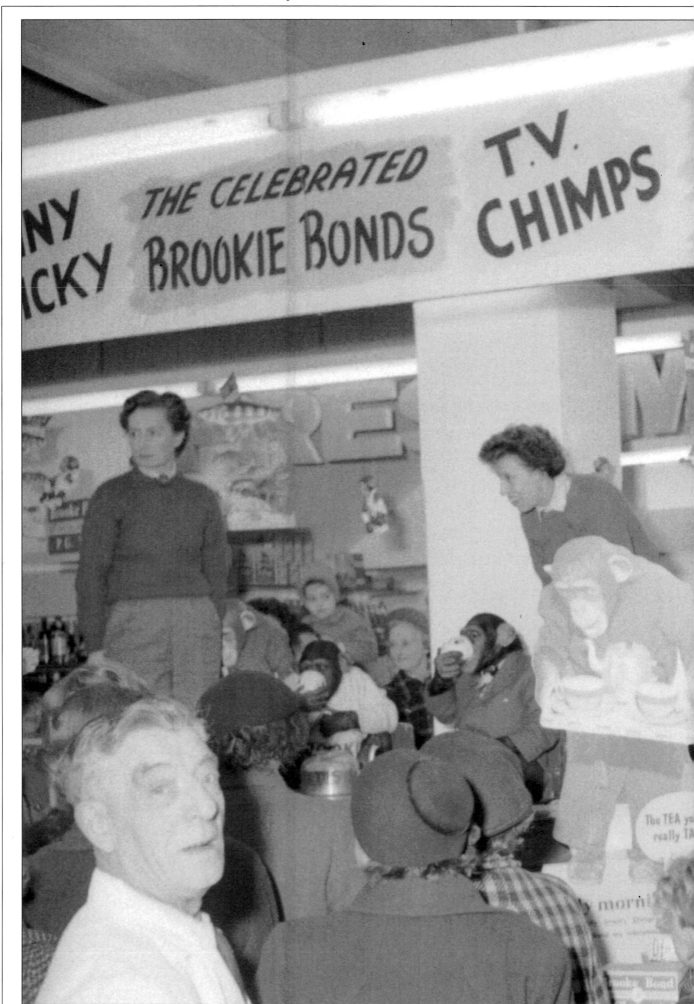

A long succession of chimp adverts has taken the company's advertising to the present day

A celebrity visit with a difference was made when Pinks self-service store in London Road was opened on 17th April 1960. Even the most popular DJ or pop star would have been eclipsed by the Ty-Phoo Tea Chimps, who were in town 'in person' to publicise the new store, and they drew the people of Portsmouth in their hundreds. The antics of these cute drinkers of 'The tea you can really taste' (to the last delicious drop) brought a smile to the faces of the children in the crowd - and to their parents' as well! A long succession of chimp adverts has taken the company's advertising up to the present day - though one advert stands out among the rest. Who can possibly forget the chimpanzee removal men shifting furniture? 'Do you know the piano's on my foot?' became a bit of a catchphrase, inevitably followed by 'You hum it son, and I'll play it!' Magic.

On the move

Trolley buses arrived in 1934 and the last tram ran on 10th November 1936

In a scene that is virtually unrecognisable today, two of Portsmouth's picturesque but draughty trams wait at the ornate tram shelter near the railway station, seen in the background, to take on more passengers, perhaps at the end of a working day. We have no date for this marvellous old photograph, but the uniforms of the menfolk in the scene indicate the years of the first world war. There are few private cars in the scene; pedal power was 'in', as was shanks' pony, though the overwhelming choice of the people was public transport - which back then meant the tram.

Imagine how wet and uncomfortable these open-top vehicles would be on rainy days! The tram drivers were even worse off than the passengers, as trams had no windscreens until the late 1930s, by which time Portsmouth had a fleet of trolley buses to offer them a far warmer ride. Tram drivers were provided with leather aprons as protection from the weather, but we can imagine what a comfortless job tram driving would have been in a harsh winter! Trolley buses arrived in 1934, and the last tram - car number 106, ran on 10th November 1936. Interestingly, the tram on the right is car number one.

Snapped in May 1959, we can see that traffic levels in Milton Road were on the increase - the thin end of the wedge. Many drivers were still hanging on to their old cars, though by that time changes in car design were imminent. Mudguards and running boards like those on the 'sit up and beg' design of the Standard 10 turning into Velder Avenue (bearing a Greater London registration) were set to become a thing of the past; headlights would be faired-in and incorporated

into sleeker body lines, flashing indicators would replace the semaphore type (remember how easy it was to forget them and leave them sticking out?), and even quarter-light windows would gradually disappear from our cars.

Linington's, well known locally as Renault dealers, today occupy the site of the BP filling station on the right; just passing the establishment, another learner driver is preparing to join the elite who have already passed their test.

'A gallon of two-star please, Mister!' Determined to switch from pedal-power to horse-power, the little chap in the ultra modern car prepares for a trip up the A3. In contrast, the wide mudguards and running boards of the old Austin behind him are a badge of a previous era of motoring; even its colour - black - was fast being replaced by colours of every hue.

The Fratton Bridge Garage where so many of us filled up with petrol in the 1960s was serving National petrol at the time. Those were the days when self service garages were just being introduced, and more mature readers will remember with nostalgia the time when you could drive your car into a petrol station and not only have the services of attendants who filled up your tank, but who also cleaned your windscreen and asked if you needed oil. In 1960 petrol was four and sevenpence halfpenny a gallon (had the word 'litre' entered the English dictionary?), though a year later the price rose by a further threepence owing to an increase in purchase tax.

All at sea!

This page: It was a sunny summer day when this view of South Parade Pier was captured for posterity. The beach and the promenade show us that Southsea was still a popular venue, though the tightly packed crowds of the 1920s and 30s are gone and the families who have taken their deck chairs on to the beach have a certain amount of breathing space around them *(bottom)*. Though a police officer stood on point duty that day, the level of traffic is not great - the two Morris Minor 1000s in the photograph, one of them a Traveller, and an A55 Cambridge moving in the opposite direction, tell us that this was the early 1960s. During the summer season the theatre offered visitors and residents alike the prospect of a great night out, and audiences were treated to shows which featured well-known personalities such as Alfred Marks, Harry Secombe, Tommy Fields, Arthur Askey and Mike and Bernie Winters. The 1954 Guide informs us that Sunday evening entertainment was provided by 'well-known stage and recording bands', and these concerts were extremely popular *(below left)*. There were few vacant seats at this particular concert; a large band was performing as a photographer snapped this scene, and across the front of the stage a banner announces the 'Miss Southsea contest - sponsored by "The News"'. We can speculate that the contest between the young bathing beauties could be about to begin. The pier was the venue for a multitude of different types of entertainment, from talent contests and community singing to open air dancing and fireworks displays. The fun never seemed to end, even while visitors were having a meal in the cafe. There, the resident organist Gordon Banner played popular music on the £3,000 organ. The pier seen here replaced the original structure, which was burnt down in 1904. Interestingly, when the 'new' pier was built a gang of 800 men were hired for a day to test its strength by jumping around on it! One hopes (but doesn't expect) that they were paid danger money! Sadly, the pier was itself doomed to suffer the same fate as the old one when fire swept through the structure as it was being used as a setting for the Ken Russell film 'Tommy'.

During the second world war, the Royal Garrison was one of the 30 churches in Portsmouth to be damaged or destroyed

Readers can play 'spot the landmark' using this marvellous eagle's-eye view of old Portsmouth, which probably dates from sometime in the 1950s. How many of them were among the workforce at Camber Docks when Vospers provided work for several hundred Portsmouth men? More than one or two, we imagine. Towards the top right, a sharp eye will pick out the shell of the Royal Garrison church. The history of the church is very ancient; we know that as far back as 1212 a hospital was founded on this spot. With 'Domus Dei' (God's House) as its principle, we know that the aim of its founders was to serve God as well as mankind. During the second world war, the Royal Garrison was one of the 30 churches in Portsmouth which were badly damaged or destroyed. A bomb hit the nave of the church in 1941; instead of being demolished, however, the shell of the building was left to stand and was preserved as an ancient monument. On The Point, bottom right, those who are in the know will immediately spot the Still & West pub, still providing refreshment to a new generation of Portmuthians, with the Customs House nearby.

Left: After a wonderful day out, hundreds of tired but satisfied holidaymakers leave the pleasure steamer to make their way back to their various 'digs'; a leisure cruise was a vital part of every family's fortnight's holiday. Where had they been, we wonder? To the Isle of Wight, perhaps, to spend a day in Ryde, with its wide, tree-lined esplanade and its long sandy beach? Or to Cowes, the main centre of yachting in Britain? The Hamble River cruise was another firm favourite - enjoyed purely for its scenic beauty back in 1938, the date of this photograph. Bursledon's fame as the fictional 'Tarrant', where the BBC's yachting saga 'Howard's Way' was set, lay far in the future at the time, as did the 'silver screen' in the corner of everyone's living room. Introduced in 1985, the 'Dynasty' style soap had by the October of that year reached number 12 in the popularity charts and was watched by 12.7 million viewers. It has been suggested that the vessel in this photograph might itself be the Isle of Wight ferry, marked out by its red and black funnel. Some reader who is 'in the know' will doubtless write and let us know!

Above: This lively scene of Portsmouth Harbour was taken from The Point in Old Portsmouth on a sunny day back in 1957. In the foreground, the Isle of Wight car ferry is on its way in, giving the onlookers on shore something interesting to watch, while in the background, near the railway station, other steamers bound for the same destination await yet another load of passengers. The Dockyard, much bombed during the second world war, dominates the far background, with the Semaphore Tower - still a familiar landmark today - towards the left. During the 19th century, the tower was the nerve centre of the Royal Dockyard, and ship movements and every other aspect of the yard's work was directed from its offices. Semaphore arms mounted on a mast at the top of the tower could pass a message from Portsmouth to the Admiralty in Whitehall along a line of connecting signal stations in around 15 minutes.

Yacht racing has always been a big draw for spectators and photographers alike, and as almost every eye is turned towards the sea, these onlookers are quite unaware that their back view is forming the foreground in the viewfinder of someone's camera. At least one lady, caught in a most unflattering pose, would no doubt have changed her stance, had she known! Had she ever seen the resulting photograph, she could at least have taken comfort from the fact that her face (and thus her identity) is quite hidden! Coats, scarves, and fur collars are called for on what was obviously a cool and windy day. Hats, of course, were worn in winter and summer alike back in the 1930s, and few people would have dreamed of being seen out of doors bare-headed. Fur was widely worn at the time, a bit of a status symbol for those who could afford to indulge themselves. In the days before the tide of public opinion began to swing against the wearing of fur, the word 'genuine' was a description to be proud of, and often the head and tail of the unfortunate animal underlined the fact that a collar was real and not artificial fur. A whole world away from the changed values of today!

> *While escorting a convoy during the war HMS Newcastle was struck by a torpedo but lived to fight another day*

Above: The second world war was a recent memory to these Portmuthians, pictured here during the 1950s, and the sight of the Southampton class cruiser HMS Newcastle in the Solent could not fail to stir patriotic pride. The Newcastle, new at the time, had taken part in the Coronation Review of 1937, and not long after that was plunged into active service with the Home Fleet. Accompanying convoys of ships was her job during the early years of the war. Cruisers such as the Newcastle did all in their power to protect their ships from attack, but time and again the unseen enemy evaded detection and stuck with deadly effect. By June 1942 the Newcastle was operating in the Eastern Mediterranean, and soon it was her own turn. While escorting a convoy, she was struck by a torpedo from a German E-boat. The gallant cruiser survived, however, and lived to fight another day. After World War II, HMS Newcastle served in another arena of war in Korea during the early 1950s. This was the last time she would see service, however; when these passers-by leaned on the fortifications to watch her pass, the Newcastle was nearing the end of her life. She was broken up in 1959.

Events of the 1960s

MELODY MAKERS

The 1960s: those were the days when the talented blues guitarist Jimi Hendrix shot to rock stardom, a youthful Cliff Richard charmed the nation with his 'Congratulations' and Sandie Shaw won the Eurovision Song Contest for Britain with 'Puppet on a String'. It was the combined musical talents of a group of outrageous working-class Liverpool lads, however, who formed the Beatles and took the world by storm with music that ranged from the experimental to ballads such as 'Yesterday'.

INVENTION AND TECHNOLOGY

A major step forward was made in 1960 when the laser was invented. An acronym for Light Amplification by Stimulated Emission of Radiation, the device produces a narrow beam of light that can travel for vast distances and is focused to give enormous power. Laser beams, as well as being able to carry far more information than radio waves, can also be used for surgery, cutting, drilling, welding and scores of other operations.

SCIENCE AND DISCOVERY

When the drug Thalidomide was first developed during the 1950s it was hailed as a wonder drug which would ease the distressing symptoms of pregnancy sickness. By the early 1960s the drug's terrible side effects were being discovered, when more than 3000 babies had been born with severe birth defects. Malformed limbs, defective eyes and faulty intestines were the heart-rending legacy left by Thalidomide.

South Parade Pier, along with the ice cream kiosks, cafeteria and gift shops, was seeing a brisk trade on the day this view was captured back in 1952. Already, however, the far-reaching effects of television were being felt, and the attractions of the promenade were on the wane. Photographs from the 1920s and 30s reveal tightly packed crowds taking the air on the pier, while the beach was often a sea of

humanity. So popular did the venue become that in 1885 East Southsea railway station was opened in Granada Road in response to the influx of tourists. As each train shed its load of passengers, Alhambra Road, linking the station with the promenade, became a mass of excited holidaymakers heading for the delights that

Southsea had to offer. The original pier, built in 1879, burnt down in 1904 despite its 'fireproof' label. The new pier which eventually rose from the ashes opened in 1908, and its theatre and concert hall, tea rooms, bandstand and shops were soon pulling the crowds in great numbers.

Shopping spree

This page and overleaf: Not all that many years ago, Charlotte Street market was quite a different place. A glimpse back in time shows us Charlotte Street as it was as recently as 1958, full of life and with a character of its very own.

These local housewives - interestingly, many of them more mature ladies - love a bargain as much as anyone else, and with shopping bags over their arms and a reluctant hubby in tow they browse among the well-stocked stalls. For many their shopping trip was a ritual, and week after week they would catch a bus into town and tour the market to find the best - and cheapest - apples, pears, oranges, grapefruit and bananas. Buying potatoes and tomatoes from one stall, apples and sprouts from another and perhaps cabbage and a couple of grapefruit from a third have always

been part of the fun of bargain hunting in the market. The prices charged by markets and street traders have traditionally been a few coppers cheaper than the average high street greengrocer would charge, and a weekly walk around the market could save a shilling or

two here and there, and stretch the inadequate house-keeping money a little bit further.

By 1962, the character of Charlotte Street was changing; a view taken in September 1962 reveals a scene which had far fewer market stalls and more modern buildings

(above). That same year, the Tricorn was in the planning stage, and the unusual building won an award for the design. The general public, however, had a different opinion and it became known as the ugliest building in the country.... Bit by bit, Charlotte Street

Market shrank under the shadow of new buildings, and though on Thursdays, Fridays and Saturdays you can still find it there behind the shopping precinct, the market which was once the hub of Portsmouth life has sadly become little more than a backwater.

Left: This fine display of seafood, pictured in November 1958, was typical of J A Rulf's Quality Fish House where, whether her family liked kippers for breakfast or fish cakes for tea, the housewife was spoilt for choice. And what was the free gift that she could save up her Happy Club Stamps for? A pound or two of pork sausages, perhaps (also on offer in the establishment), or a couple of jars of shellfish? The prices at Rulf's were right, from the English eggs offered at 3/6d a dozen (just less than 18 new pence) to the more expensive new laid ones on the left at 4/3d a dozen. If you wanted a change from everyday fish such as haddock, cod and mackerel, this was the place to go; bream, skate, bloaters - all were among this marvellous display. And if you were counting the pennies you could even buy whale meat, a bargain at 1/9d lb, if you liked that kind of thing. And when you'd got it, prominently displayed recipes for baked fish and stuffed fish told you how to cook it. Marvellous stuff.

Above: Do you remember collecting Green Shield Stamps? Opening day at the new Green Shield shop in Kingston Road was a popular occasion, and defying the winter cold in December 1963, a queue of avid collectors has formed outside the door. What a pity we can only read part of the sign on the window; clearly a number of free stamps were on offer to the first-comers.

The little green stamps were highly popular during the 1960s and 70s, and were given to customers on a range of different goods by hundreds of stores and garages. Remember how week by week we stuck them carefully in their little books until we had a nice little stack of them? Then came the red letter day, when we had filled enough books to take along to the shop and exchange them for gifts, which could be anything from a handbag to a set of kitchen scales or mixing bowls. Exactly when Green Shield Stamps disappeared from the scene is not recalled. Perhaps some reader will be able to pinpoint the date.

The family with a pharmaceutical formula for success

When Percy Gordon Tremlett first opened the doors of his very own chemist's shop at number 2a Fratton Road in 1901, he could not have known that, a hundred years later and three generations on, the family name would still be above the doors of chemist shops throughout Portsmouth. Originally from the Isle of Wight, Percy had come to Fratton, Portsmouth, to serve a three-year apprenticeship with pharmacists Brews & Mackintosh, and after qualifying he decided to remain in Portsmouth. The local community came to rely on Tremlett's to bring relief from a wide range of aches and ailments; few families could afford to call out the doctor except in cases of real emergency,

and instead they would consult their local chemist, who would use their scientific knowledge, coupled with considerable ingenuity, to dispense medicine and good advice and, with a bit of luck, cure every conceivable problem. Percy worked not only as a dispensing chemist, but also as an optician and dentist; Tremlett's was equipped with various awesome items of optical and dental apparatus, including a foot-operated drilling machine which stood next to the dentist's chair. And from 1925 onwards the people of Fratton were also able to benefit from the services of Percy's son, Richard Gordon Tremlett, who began his apprenticeship in his father's shop in that year, at the age of 18. Pharmaceutical training had changed little since the days of his father's apprenticeship. Laudanum, opium, and quinine were widely used in the dispensary. Each dispensing chemist had their own proprietary 'special formula' cough and tonic mixtures, the composition of which was a closely-guarded secret, and these would be sold in the shop, together with such items as tooth powders - again, of their own concoction - various salts, powders, and pills, poppy heads which would be boiled up with chamomile flowers as a toothache remedy, and toiletries such as soap, toilet rolls and hot water bottles. And on the counter stood a tank of leeches, which were widely used to suck out the bad blood which was causing the problem.

The life of the early 20th century pharmacist was clearly not lacking in colour, and Richard took to the profession with as much enthusiasm as his father had. Changes were afoot, however, and in 1927 it was decreed that pharmacies must choose to be either a dispenser of medicines, an optician or a dentist - they could no longer be all three. Percy chose to be a pharmacist, a choice with which his son fully concurred. In due course Richard married and opened his own pharmacy shop at number 1, New Road East, Copnor; father and son each continued to manage their own business until 1934, when Percy Tremlett fell ill. Richard then took control of his father's shop as well as his own, and kept the business going throughout the war years. Tremlett's was the only pharmacy to stay open in the evening during that period, and to satisfy the vigilant eyes of the Air Raid Wardens a double blackout curtain was rigged up in the doorway, the idea being when you entered the shop you went through the first one and closed it behind you before opening the second - or vice versa to come out. Fratton suffered its share of damage during the air raids, with the goods yard being a bomb target, but Tremlett's itself escaped unharmed.

At the end of war Richard acquired a third shop at number 117, Winter Road, Southsea. The post-war years brought a number of changes in the pharmaceutical profession. Scientific advances had improved the range of drugs available; penicillin, first developed as an antibiotic in 1940, became available as a injection, although a course of five injections at

Left: The interior of Tremletts Chemist in the late 1950s. Below: Fratton Road in 1926 with Tremletts Chemist shop to the left of the picture.

ten shillings a shot was barely affordable for the average family. The National Health Act set out to solve this problem by making medicine free to everybody. This altered the relationship between doctor, pharmacist and patients, as doctors, who had formerly done much of their own dispensing, now left it to the pharmacist.

In 1947 the Tremlett's business was incorporated as a limited liability company. The new company was named Tremlett (Chemists) Limited, and three directors were appointed: Richard Tremlett himself, his mother Annie May Tremlett, and Kenneth Frederick Allen, who was the family solicitor. Then in 1952 a separate company, R G Tremlett Ltd was incorporated, with Richard and his wife Molly Doreen as joint directors. This signalled the beginning of a period of expansion for both the family companies, and in fact a third family enterprise began in 1974 when Ian Tremlett purchased the New Road East business, which he carried on under the name of Tempo Drug Store. Tremletts (Chemists) and R G Tremlett each built up a network of pharmacies and other premises, readers may remember the Tremlett name appearing above various shops in and around Portsmouth - Queen's Parade, other premises in Fratton Road, and 20 West Street, Porchester; this latter branch subsequently

Top: A night-time view of Tremletts Chemists in the 1970s.

moved to 44 West Street. In 1984 the family business was re-structured; the company formerly known as R G Tremlett now became Tremletts Chemists Ltd and operated as the trading company for the group. The former Tremletts (Chemists) Ltd became the holding company and was renamed Tremlett Holdings Ltd. The following year Tremletts Chemists set the trend for the expansion which has continued through to the present day by taking over the business of Bridgemary Pharmacies Ltd of 182 Nobles Avenue, Bridgemary, Gosport.

"Spiders were boiled up into a sort of cough mixture and they used to drink it."

Tremlett's has remained a family business to this day. Molly Tremlett, the late Richard's wife and the daughter-in-law of the founder, has witnessed the growth of the firm from one shop into the thriving concern which it is today; at the time of writing Molly is living in Portsmouth and looking forward to her 90th birthday in the year 2000. Current managing directors of Tremlett Chemists Ltd are Bill and Ian Tremlett, grandsons of Percy, and the fourth generation is represented by Dr Helen Tremlett, Bill's daughter, who is employed by the business as a locum pharmacist. Helen's training was no doubt very different from that which her great grandfather received during his apprenticeship, a century ago, and no doubt these changes have been good for our health. However, the more colourful, if rather less exact science of the pharmacist in bygone times is not without its appeal - now that we no longer have to depend upon it - and we will conclude this article with a few fascinating extracts from Mr Richard Tremlett's booklet entitled Sixty-Two Years A Fratton Pharmacist. Richard Tremlett, as well as being an extremely astute businessman, was clearly a great character with a wonderful sense of humour, and his leaflet gives an invaluable and often entertaining insight not only into the technical skills of the pharmacist but also into life in Portsmouth during the early years of the family business.

'All through my apprenticeship days there was an old man with a whistle pipe called Piccolo Pete, and at ten o'clock every Monday morning, rain or shine, he started outside our shop and marched three or four hundred yards up Fratton Road and back again. Then he went back again picking up 6d in each shop.'

'People had very little money in those days and it was not unusual for small boys to be sent in saying "Can you change this toilet roll for a bar of soap as the visitors have not turned up."'

'All they had in those days were a few drugs and if Sodium Bicarb didn't cure you they just doubled the dose. A lot of "faith in your Doctor" came into the treatment.'

'You were in trouble if the Chief Pharmacist, on examining a Batch of Pills, said, "Which one does the patient take first, the large or the small?"'

'Mr Arkell's (Mr Arkell was another chemist in the city) son used to tell me how they made "worm oil" - a pound of garden worms was put into a large earthenware jar of olive oil, sealed off and buried in the garden for a year - strained off and got prescribed for all kinds of ailments.'

'Spiders were boiled up into a sort of cough mixture and they used to drink it.'

'Every Saturday night all the children in Fratton had either a dose of Syrup of Figs or Brimstone (Sulphur) and Treacle. What happened on Sundays boggles the imagination.'

'The leech . . . sucked out the blood until it was distended. It was then removed . . . and placed in a glass of salt solution, when it disgorged the blood and was put back in the tank again for further use.'

However nostalgic we may feel when we look at old photographs of chemists' shops, with their wonderful array of nicely-shaped bottles in the window and those mysterious names on the labels, next time you visit Tremlett's and survey the well-stocked shelves, you may be secretly glad that times have moved on: effective, pleasant-tasting modern remedies, highly-qualified staff - and not a leech, spider or earthworm in sight!

Below: A 1990s view of the interior of the Chemist.

One hundred years in the driving seat - and still out in front

Frederick Adolphus Hendy little dreamed, when he opened his bicycle and outdoor clothing shop in Whitchurch back in 1859, that his fledgling business was destined to be the acorn from which the great oak of the Hendy Lennox Group would grow. Those, after all, were the gentle days of horsemanship, pedal power and shanks' pony, 26 years before Karl Benz invented the first petrol driven car, and nearly 50 years before Henry Ford's Model T began to roll off the assembly line.

Frederick concentrated on selling his own branded bicycles which he assembled in his shop from pre-manufactured parts. Within a short time he found that the shop was too small, and with his wife and five children he made a key move to larger premises in Southampton. The bicycle and tricycle business took off, and became a limited company in 1898. Shortly after that, Frederick diversified into four-wheeled transport, taking on agencies for Benz and Bolle - an unusual step for a bicycle dealer to take, as it was the blacksmiths and carriage builders who were making the transition to selling motor cars.

It was Frederick's son Percy who in 1910 took the bold step of signing an agreement with Henry Ford

Right: The Southsea premises pictured circa 1948. Below: An interior view of the Southsea workshop, 1948.

himself, making the Hendy Group the first official Ford Main Dealer in Great Britain. The Model T, or 'Tin Lizzie', lived up to Ford's - and Percy's - expectations. Hendy's also dealt in Ford commercial vehicles, and the company grew rapidly. In 1913 Hendy's opened a new branch in Palmerston Road, Bournemouth; the venture was successful and a year later another branch was opened in Southsea.

The outbreak of war brought with it a change of direction in the company, and Hendy's became responsible for the maintenance and servicing of the Fordson tractors, vital to the nation's food production. When peace was restored, so was the popularity of the Model T, though the price had risen steeply from £115 before the war to £220.

factory in Northam was bombed. Hendy's had the own wartime casualties; in Southampton the Pound Tree Road building was unfortunately destroyed in an air raid.

When World War II ended in 1945 it took a number of years before the motor trade returned to normal. The launch of the new Consul and Zephyr Six at the 1950 Earls Court Motor Show marked the beginnings of a new Ford range, and these two successful models were joined by the Anglia and Prefect in 1953. By the time Hendy's celebrated their 50th anniversary in 1959 the Group was also operating as Gordon Motors in Cosham, Portsmouth - a development made in 1956 - and had extended both its Chandlers Ford and the Vincent Walk premises. When Percy Hendy died in 1956 the company passed into the hands of his nephew Arthur.

Over the following 50 years the Hendy Group grew beyond all expectations, and Hendy Ford today is established as a leading car dealership throughout the region. The tradition of success is strong within the Hendy Group; the company has proved time and again that it is quick to recognise a good opportunity and flexible enough to adapt, so although it is impossible to predict exactly what the next 50 years will bring, there can be no doubt that the Hendy Group can look forward to a bright future.

Top left: The Cosham showroom circa 1958.
Above left: Hendy Body, Farlington, Portsmouth.
Below: Hendy Ford, Cosham.

Between 1914 and 1938 Hendy's saw real expansion. Percy Hendy Ltd was formed in 1923, and the same year saw Frederick W Hendy appointed as company chairman, and the Bournemouth branch became the Ford Main Dealer as Hendy Bros Ltd. In Southampton the company made several moves, establishing a main headquarters, a motor-cycle and accessory showroom, a tractor sales department and a bicycle retail and wholesale venture by the name of Accessories (Southampton) Ltd. In 1938 - just a year before Britain was once more at war - a further new site was opened in Chandlers Ford.

The war years were difficult ones for everyone involved in the motor trade. The Palmerston Road branch continued with truck and car servicing and also acted as a Ministry of Supply Auxiliary Workshop; meanwhile the Chandlers Ford and Vincent's Walk, Southampton branches were requisitioned by the Ministry of Aircraft Production and were used as Spitfire factories when Supermarine's

Zurich, covering the risks

Zurich in the UK celebrated its 75th anniversary in 1997, and it's difficult given the size of the company now, to imagine the small beginnings from which it came. The infant enterprise started with a lone pioneer - the aptly named WS Work - who was given the task of laying the foundations from which today's highly successful organisation has grown.

Starting without even an office from which to work, he set to with a will. His immediate concern was to overcome the prejudice against foreign companies at a time when competition in the insurance world was particularly intense. Patriotism was running high in the aftermath of the first world war, and people everywhere were being encouraged to buy British.

Zurich's first office back in 1922, was based in London. The first premium paid was for the princely sum of 17 shillings and sixpence (just over 87p in decimal money) for public liability insurance for CH Lever. The whole of the first year's business amounted to only £84 from a dozen policies. But steadily income increased, and by 1925 the company was feeling confident enough to acquire a firm, Lancashire and Cheshire Insurance Company, which was in liquidation.

An important and very successful business relationship for Zurich, also initiated in 1925, was that with the Ford Motor Company. This was based on an innovative idea that all vehicles should be covered at the same premium regardless of horsepower or value. It was an

*Right: Victory House on the edge of Portsmouth Harbour was Zurich Insurance's UK Head Office between 1970 and 1977. **Below:** Mr Fritz Gerber who went on to become Chairman of the Zurich Group, pictured with the Lord Mayor of Portsmouth, Alderman W J Evans, at the opening of Victory House on April 23, 1970.*

outstanding, long-term success. Ford remained an important contact for Zurich to the extent that in the early 1960s, when the new-look Ford Anglia was introduced, Zurich's Dublin office were besieged by queues of motorists desperate to arrange cover.

The company was in good condition at the outbreak of the second world war, but a direct hit to their London office (Fairfax House) in 1940 meant that the company had to evacuate staff out of the City. Staff were relocated to Minsterworth in Gloucestershire. Any idea of gracious living quickly disappeared when they found themselves sleeping either four or six to a room/dormitory, with curtained-off cubicles and shared washbasins.

The move to Portsmouth

Space was at a premium after the war and, with Britain becoming more prosperous during the 1950s and business consequently brisker than ever, pressure remained high with the office beginning to bulge at the seams. In 1968, the Swiss Head Office agreed to the UK Manager's wish to move all administrative and service departments out of London to Portsmouth.

Zurich's first home in Portsmouth was a newly-completed 12-storey office block within a stone's throw of Portsmouth's historic dockyard, in the area known as The Hard. There was some surprise and delight when the company announced that the building would be known as Victory House rather than Zurich House as was expected. Mr AF Noyes, UK General Manager at the time, explained "We have decided to pay a compliment to our hosts, the City of Portsmouth, and associate ourselves with the great naval tradition of the place." Zurich's association with Britain was further endorsed by the choice of St George's Day for the official opening.

The move proved successful in every way - high initial costs were recouped within three years. Key people willingly transferred to Portsmouth, and the company steadily recruited hundreds of local people, contributing to the area's economy. By 1977, the company had moved yet again into the prestigious 15 storey Zurich House, which was purpose-built opposite Portsmouth's main railway station.

The future continues to look good for Zurich. Over the last couple of years they launched a new company logo and image - the Z with a smile. In September 1998, the new Group was born when the Zurich Group merged with the financial services businesses of B A T Industries. The Group includes some other famous names - Allied Dunbar, Eagle Star, Farmers and Scudder Kemper, to mention a few. A new Group with over thirty million customers in more than 60 countries worldwide. Zurich now has in excess of 68,000 employees working in over 50 countries. On December 31st 1998, the Group had USD 415 billion of assets under management.

The company's vision is to be world class for customers, shareholders and employees through the techniques of the four core businesses - non-life and life insurance, reinsurance and asset management. There seems no reason, based on their history to doubt they will achieve world class status.

Top: *The topping-out ceremony of Victory House in 1969. The masts of Nelson's celebrated flagship, HMS Victory can be seen in the background.*
Above left: *Zurich House, Portsmouth.*

Taking The Bridge Centre into the future

Can you believe that it's little more than a decade since The Bridge Shopping Centre opened? The eleventh of May, 1989, was the day when the people of Portsmouth thronged the streets to watch a spectacular procession make its way along Arundel Street and into Fratton Road. The T S Tenacity marching band accompanied the Whitbread dray pulled by the Shire horses, and a miniature fire engine. After the official opening of The Bridge Shopping Centre, the crowds rushed eagerly through the Centre's revolving doors - a novelty in themselves at that time. Inside, they discovered a shoppers' paradise of 25 separate stores under one roof, covering all the essentials and more besides - clothes, shoes, sportswear and equipment, videos, CD's, food, banking facilities, a Post Office, and even a cafe. For the first time Fratton's shoppers could wander from shop to shop along the Mall in a draught-free, air-conditioned environment, stop for a break and a chat, have a cup of coffee and a snack or even a main meal. When they felt suitably refreshed they could get up and shop some more - and all without getting their feet wet, even on the rainiest of days!

Right: *The ladieswear department in the late 1940s.* **Below:** *The Co-operative Store on Fratton Road at the end of the 19th century.*

The Centre was designed to be easily accessible to everybody - car users, bus and rail travellers, pedestrians, wheelchair users and mothers with prams. The Fratton Road entrance, which leads directly into the shopping mall, is on the main bus route, and is just five minutes' walk from the railway station. Access for motorists is equally convenient with the modern network of motorways and link roads. Motorists can fill up at the purpose-built petrol station attached to the complex. Parking space in the Centre's own car park is generous, with room for 400 cars and with designated bays next to the entrance reserved for the disabled.

Shoppers were, of course, already accustomed to shopping on this particular spot, as the new Centre was built on the site of the former Co-op House Department Store. The Co-operative's 100-year connection with trading on this particular spot was not lost when the new complex was created, as The Bridge Shopping Centre was home to the Society's new Bridge Superstore.

The history of the Portsea Island Mutual Co-operative Society Limited, dates right back to 1873; however, one incident which is of particular relevance to this site, and which may well have been brought back into the minds of some of the more mature shoppers by the presence of the miniature fire engine No. 5 in the procession of May 1989, was a devastating fire which broke out at Co-op House on 20th July 1934. The cause of the fire was never discovered, but resulted in the almost total destruction of the Co-op's central premises. Rebuilding began almost immediately and was completed in 1936.

So the past has carried forward into the present with the continuation of retail activity on this site; and the present will be carried forward into the future, because buried in the foundations, beneath the flooring in the mall as it stretches back from the Fratton Road entrance, lies a time capsule which was sealed and placed there in 1989, and which contains details of contemporary life in Portsmouth together with certain items in general use. It is unlikely that any of us who are around at the time of reading this book will ever see the contents of the capsule, as the date set for its opening is May 2089, but it is nice to know that when the time comes future generations will think back to the people who created The Bridge Shopping Centre, a hundred years ago.

At the opening ceremony, Mr Jim Palmer of Mutual Associates Limited, the developers responsible for bringing us The Bridge Shopping Centre, told the assembled crowds that he hoped they would 'find here the range and variety of shopping that appeals to you.' We certainly did; a decade later, although our requirements have altered, we still rely on The Bridge Centre to provide us with what we want and trust that when the time capsule is opened The Bridge will hold every bit as much appeal for the shoppers of the 21st century - however many tastes in clothes, food and entertainment may have changed by then!

Top left: *Fire destroyed the Fratton Road store in July 1934.*
Top right: *Co-op House and Fratton Road celebrate the Queen's Silver Jubilee in 1977.*
Left: *Crowds gather at the opening of the new Bridge Shopping Centre on Fratton Road in May 1989.*

Putting a roof over the heads of those in need

Having a roof over our heads is all many of us ask for. Yet circumstances can combine to make even this seem an impossible dream. Portsmouth, for all its excellent qualities, features high on the national Index of Deprivation, with some postcodes in the poorest one per cent. Many statistics have been compiled, many sociological theories expounded, and much legislation introduced; but what matters most to the people behind the statistics is practical help, such as has been forthcoming from the Portsmouth Housing Association.

Since its foundation more than 25 years ago, the PHA has done a tremendous amount to improve life for the more vulnerable groups within the community - the elderly, the unemployed, ex-offenders and those with learning disabilities. The Association took in its first tenant in 1975; three years later it was providing accommodation for 100 people, and the number of homes available has continued to grow year upon year. Today the PHA Group, of which Portsmouth Housing Association is the founder and 'parent' member, provides a wide range of services. Accommodation takes the form of purpose-built as well as restored, converted and refurbished properties, and includes flats for the elderly, hostels for young, single and homeless people, and Wintershelters for those sleeping rough. With the emphasis on Best Value, the Group works closely with its residents, holding regular consultations; it also offers expert independent advice to individuals, together with specialised services - such as support for vulnerable residents, support to families in accommodation crisis, and debt counselling - based on its in-depth understanding of the often complex issues surrounding housing, homelessness and benefit problems. The Group is committed to meeting the needs of the local community. In addition to the rented housing provided by Portsmouth Housing Association, low-cost home ownership is offered by Southlands Housing Association. The Group also participates in community and economic regeneration projects; it takes part in debates, enquiries, reviews and fact-finding exercises. The Group works closely with local government and other interested bodies, raising housing issues and launching initiatives such as the innovative Train & Build project to provide training opportunities for the area's long-term unemployed.

Committed to equal opportunities and co-operative working, Portsmouth Housing Association is concerned with real needs and is strongly rooted in the local communities. It will continue working with people in the area, enabling them not just to get a decent home but also to develop their own confidence and skills. For 25 years PHA has been working towards an improvement in quality of life and long-term opportunities for people in need. Its success in the past has make life better for many Portsmouth people. Its continuing success in the future will give new hope to many more.

Above: *Rev Bill Sargent, local vicar and one of the founders of PHA Group outside 43 Daulston Road, PHA's first house.* **Below:** *The Portsmouth Foyer providing accommodation and employment support for young people.*

Fratton Road with the 165ft-high tower of St Mary's standing tall on the skyline

The bathing pool was a popular feature of the Southsea summer season, and the charge of three-pence included swimming instruction, the use of the nearby playground, and deckchairs for the parents

Acknowledgments

The publishers are grateful to Ron Forrest and to Bob Irwin of JA Hewes Photographers of Southsea for allowing the reproduction of images from their collections.
The kindness and patience of these local gentlemen went far beyond the call of duty and we are delighted to recognise their contribution here.

Thanks are also due to
Peggy Burns who penned the editorial text
and Margaret Wakefield for her copywriting skills